THE ONE YEAR *Devotional Guide*

The ONE YEAR® Devotional Guide

Tyndale House
Publishers, Inc.
Wheaton, Illinois

Visit Tyndale's exciting Web site at www.tyndale.com

New Living, The One Year, and the New Living Translation logo are registered trademarks of Tyndale House Publishers, Inc.

Edited by Shawn Harrison
Cover designed by Ron Kaufmann
Interior designed by Timothy R. Botts

ISBN 0-8423-3546-3
Printed in the United States of America

05 04 03 02 01 00 99
 9   8   7   6   5   4   3   2

FOREWORD

*Think of ways to encourage one another
to outbursts of love and good deeds.*   Hebrews 10:24

Do you struggle to read the Bible consistently?
Have you wondered how to inspire a group to read the Bible together?

It can be hard to read the Bible consistently. But you can put God's
Word at the center of your life! Let *The One Year Bible* lead you
through the entire Bible this year, and use *The One Year Bible Study
Guide* to enrich your Bible reading on a weekly basis.

The One Year Bible Study Guide is an ideal tool for encouraging
your family, small group, or Sunday school class to read the Bible
together. When you meet, use the guide to encourage each other in
your Bible reading and as a starting place for discussion. It's also a
great guide for personal weekly reflection. Use the guide to review
and reflect on your reading from the previous week.

Each weekly study includes four parts:

- **The *Combined Readings* list gives you the Scriptures
  covered each week.** This makes it easy to use the study guide
  with your personal Bible if you so choose.

- **The *Bible Memory Challenge* suggests great verses for
  you to memorize.** Choose a passage or two to memorize from
  the list each week. (You could use the study guide for four years,
  memorizing a different set of passages each year.) If you are
  meeting with a small group, quiz each other on the memory
  passages.

- **The *Pop Quiz* offers review questions for each week's
  readings.** At the end of each week, either individually or in your
  group, review your reading with the Pop Quiz. Use it to keep
  everyone in your group reading!

- **The *Weekly Reflection* provides relevant thoughts and
  questions on an important passage.** Use this for your own
  personal study or to lead your small group Bible study. Ask the
  discussion questions to get everyone in the group involved.

It is our prayer that *The One Year Bible* and *The One Year Bible Study Guide* will help you get into God's Word in the coming year and for many years to come.

The Publisher

INDEX OF TOPICS
in the Weekly Reflections

COMBINED READINGS

Genesis 1:1–19:38
Matthew 1:1–7:14
Psalm 1:1–8:9
Proverbs 1:1–2:15

BIBLE MEMORY CHALLENGE

Genesis 15:6
Matthew 5:3-12
Psalm 1:1-6
Proverbs 1:7

POP QUIZ

OT: Why were Adam and Eve banished from the Garden of Eden? (Gen. 3:22-24)

OT: Why did Noah build a huge boat? (Gen. 6:11-22)

OT: When was the first rainbow, and what did it mean? (Gen. 9:13-17)

OT: Why was the world's first great building project never completed? (Gen. 11:1-9)

NT: How did Joseph become convinced not to break his engagement with Mary? (Matt. 1:18-25)

NT: Why did Herod want the wise men to tell him where the newborn king was? (Matt. 2:1-16)

NT: According to Jesus, why should his disciples forgive others? (Matt. 6:14-15)

NT: Why should Jesus' disciples not worry about their everyday needs, and what should they think about instead? (Matt. 6:25-33)

Psalms: What are those who delight in the Lord compared to? (1:3)

Proverbs: What is the purpose of the proverbs? (1:2-4)

I Believe

topic: Belief

reading: Genesis 15:1-21

verse: Abram believed the Lord, and the Lord declared him righteous because of his faith. (Genesis 15:6)

We have read of Abram's mistakes, and we know he was only human. Though sinful, Abram believed and trusted in God. It was faith, not actions, that made Abram right with God. We, too, can have a right relationship with God by believing in him. Our outward actions—church attendance, prayer, good deeds—will not make us right with God. It is also important to recognize that our mistakes do not separate us from God's love. A right relationship is based on faith—the belief that God is who he says he is and does what he says he will do.

? Why do we naturally tend to think our actions are more important than our basic beliefs?

? How are our beliefs and behaviors connected?

? What impresses you most about Abram's belief in God?

? What keeps people from believing in God?

? When have you struggled most with your religious beliefs?

COMBINED READINGS
Genesis 20:1–32:12
Matthew 7:15–11:6
Psalm 9:1–13:6
Proverbs 2:16–3:18

BIBLE MEMORY CHALLENGE
Genesis 22:15-18
Matthew 7:21
Psalm 9:1
Proverbs 3:5-6

POP QUIZ

OT: Who wept at thinking her son would die of thirst in the desert? (Gen. 21:14-16)

OT: How did God test Abraham's faith and obedience? (Gen. 22:1-2)

OT: How did Jacob obtain his father's blessing? (Gen. 27:1-29)

OT: How did Laban get Jacob to marry Leah first instead of Rachel? (Gen. 29:22-25)

NT: To what does Jesus compare the person who builds his life on Jesus' teaching? (Matt. 7:24-27)

NT: Why did Jesus exclaim that a Roman officer had greater faith than anyone else he had met? (Matt. 8:5-13)

NT: What did Jesus say that provoked the teachers of religious law to charge him with blasphemy? (Matt. 9:1-3)

NT: Why didn't Jesus and his disciples fast? (Matt. 9:14-17)

Psalms: What were David's neighbors doing that prompted him to cry out to the Lord for help? (12:1-4)

Proverbs: Why should we follow the steps of good men? (2:20-22)

God Will Not Forsake Us

topic: Trust

reading: Psalm 9:7-10

verse: Those who know your name trust in you, for you, O Lord, have never abandoned anyone who searches for you.
(Psalm 9:10)

God will never forsake those who trust in him. To forsake someone is to abandon that person. God's promise does not mean that if we trust in him we will never experience loss or suffering; it means that God himself will never leave us. We can always count on him to be there for us.

? When have you felt abandoned by your friends or coworkers? What were you counting on them to do?

? How have you relied and counted upon the Lord for his help in your life?

? How has the Lord demonstrated in your life that he has not forsaken you?

? What would you say to someone who feels as if God has abandoned him or her?

? In what area of your life do you need to place more trust in God?

COMBINED READINGS
Genesis 32:13–45:28
Matthew 11:7–14:36
Psalm 14:1–18:50
Proverbs 3:19–4:13

BIBLE MEMORY CHALLENGE
Genesis 35:2-3
Matthew 11:28-30
Psalm 14:1-3
Proverbs 3:21-26

POP QUIZ

OT: Why was Jacob's name changed to Israel? (Gen. 32:22-32)

OT: Why did Joseph's brothers hate him? (Gen. 37:1-8)

OT: How did Joseph become Pharaoh's second in command? (Gen. 41:1-44)

OT: Who convinced Joseph not to make Benjamin a slave? (Gen. 44:18-34)

NT: Why did Jesus permit his disciples to eat on the Sabbath? (Matt. 12:1-8)

NT: How did the Pharisees respond when Jesus healed a man with a deformed hand on the Sabbath—and why did they respond that way? (Matt. 12:9-14)

NT: Why did the Pharisees and teachers of the law ask Jesus for a sign, and how did Jesus respond? (Matt. 12:38-42)

NT: What prompted Jesus to say that a prophet is honored everywhere except in his hometown? (Matt. 13:53-58)

Psalms: Who may worship in God's presence? (15:1-2)

Proverbs: Why should we make plans? (3:21-23)

Step of Faith

topic: Doubts

reading: Matthew 11:1-19

verse: God blesses those who are not offended by me. (Matthew 11:6)

*A*s John the Baptist sat in prison, he began to experience some doubts about whether Jesus was the Messiah. He sent his disciples to ask Jesus if he was really the one they were waiting for or if they should keep on looking. Jesus answered John's doubts by pointing to his acts of healing the blind, lame, and deaf; curing the lepers; raising the dead; and preaching the good news about God. If you sometimes doubt your salvation, the forgiveness of your sins, or God's work in your life, look at the evidence in Scripture and God's promises to us. Then ask the Lord to give you the faith you need to trust him more. When you doubt, don't turn away from Christ—turn to him.

? What causes people to second-guess themselves?

? When have you ever doubted God's ability or willingness to act?

? Why do you believe that Jesus is God's Son and the Savior of the world?

? How do you personally handle doubts when they come?

? Who has helped you deal with some of your doubts? How was this person helpful?

COMBINED READINGS

Genesis 46—Exodus 9:35
Matthew 15:1–19:30
Psalm 19:1–24:10
Proverbs 4:14–6:5

BIBLE MEMORY CHALLENGE

Genesis 49:10
Matthew 16:15-19
Psalm 23:1-6
Proverbs 4:23-27

POP QUIZ

OT: Why did Pharaoh subject the Hebrews to forced labor and order that all of their male babies be killed? (Exod. 1:6-16)

OT: Why did Moses flee from Egypt and go to live in Midian? (Exod. 2:11-15)

OT: How did Moses respond when God told him to go lead the Israelites out of Egypt? (Exod. 3:4–4:17)

OT: How did Pharaoh respond to the plagues that God sent on Egypt? (Exod. 7:1–9:35)

NT: Whom did Jesus call hypocrites, and why? (Matt. 15:1-9)

NT: How did the Gentile woman convince Jesus to heal her daughter? (Matt. 15:22-28)

NT: If you have faith as small as a mustard seed, what can happen? (Matt. 17:20)

NT: Who is the greatest in the Kingdom of Heaven? (Matt. 18:4)

Psalms: What tells of the glory of God? (19:1-6)

Proverbs: Why should we not cosign for a loan? (6:1-5)

Great Value

topic: Eternal Life

reading: Matthew 16:21-28

verse: How do you benefit if you gain the whole world but lose your own soul in the process? Is anything worth more than your soul? (Matthew 16:26)

*T*hose who don't know Christ live each day as if this life is all there is. In reality, this life is just the introduction to eternity. How we live this brief span determines our eternal state. What we accumulate on earth cannot purchase eternal life. Even the highest social or civic honors cannot earn for us another day of life on earth. But Christians can look forward to the hope of heaven and live each day in the light of eternity.

? How would you live differently if you knew exactly when and how you were going to die?

? When have you sacrificed immediate pleasure in order to achieve some greater good in the long run?

? If your soul is worth more than the whole world, how should that affect the way you spend your time?

? How does the promise of eternal life change the way you live every day?

? What situation in your life do you need to reevaluate from an eternal perspective?

COMBINED READINGS

Exodus 10:1–23:13
Matthew 20:1–24:28
Psalm 25:1–29:11
Proverbs 6:6–7:23

BIBLE MEMORY CHALLENGE

Exodus 20:2-17
Matthew 20:25-28
Psalm 27:1
Proverbs 6:6-11

POP QUIZ

OT: What finally broke Pharaoh's resistance so that he let the Israelites go? (Exod. 12:28-42)

OT: How did the Israelites respond when they didn't have enough food or water? (Exod. 16:1-3; 17:1-3)

OT: What wise advice did Moses' father-in-law, Jethro, give when he came to visit Moses? (Exod. 18:13-26)

OT: Where did God establish his covenant with Israel and give them the Ten Commandments? (Exod. 19:1–20:21)

NT: Why did the vineyard owner pay the workers equally? (Matt. 20:8-16)

NT: What events did Jesus predict to his twelve disciples on the way to Jerusalem? (Matt. 20:17-19)

NT: What must those who want to be leaders do, and why? (Matt. 20:26-28)

NT: What is the first and greatest commandment? (Matt. 22:37-38)

Psalms: How can we become friends with the Lord? (25:14)

Proverbs: Why is it important to work hard? (6:6-11)

Fear or Faith

topic: Attitudes

reading: Exodus 14:5-14

verse: Then they turned against Moses and complained, "Why did you bring us out here to die in the wilderness? Weren't there enough graves for us in Egypt? Why did you make us leave?" (Exodus 14:11)

*S*ix hundred Egyptian war chariots were bearing down on the helpless Israelites, who were trapped between the mountains and the sea. The Israelites thought they were doomed. After watching God's powerful hand deliver them from Egypt, their only response was fear, whining, and despair. Their lack of faith in God is startling. Yet how often do we find ourselves doing the same thing, grumbling or complaining over inconveniences or discomforts? God has given us these examples in Scripture so that we can learn to trust him the first time. By focusing on God's faithfulness in the past, we can avoid responding to a crisis with fear and complaining in the present or future.

? How do you feel when you spend time with a person who constantly complains?

? In what circumstances are you tempted to worry or complain, rather than trust in God?

? Why do you think we choose to worry and whine about our problems when we know it is better to trust in God?

? How can a positive attitude make a difficult situation easier?

? How have you been able to maintain a good attitude in bad times?

COMBINED READINGS
Exodus 23:14–35:9
Matthew 24:29–27:31
Psalm 30:1–33:22
Proverbs 7:24–9:6

BIBLE MEMORY CHALLENGE
Exodus 34:14
Matthew 26:26-28
Psalm 32:8
Proverbs 8:10-11

POP QUIZ

OT: How did the people respond when Moses had announced all the teachings and regulations from the Lord? (Exod. 24:3)

OT: For what building did God give Moses the plans, and what was the purpose of that building? (Exod. 25:8-9)

OT: How did God prepare craftsmen who would be capable of carrying out these plans? (Exod. 31:1-6)

OT: What did the Israelites do when Moses didn't come down from the mountain for forty days? (Exod. 32:1-6)

NT: What should we do to be ready for the return of the Son of Man? (Matt. 24:42-44)

NT: What did the five wise bridesmaids do? (Matt. 25:1-13)

NT: In the final judgment, who are the sheep, and who are the goats? (Matt. 25:32-46)

NT: Why did a woman pour perfume over Jesus' head during supper, and how did Jesus respond? (Matt. 26:6-13)

Psalms: How long does God's anger last? (30:5)

Proverbs: What should we choose over riches, and why? (8:10-11)

The Domino Effect

topic: Sin

reading: Exodus 34:1-17

verse: I show this unfailing love to many thousands by forgiving every kind of sin and rebellion. Even so I do not leave sin unpunished, but I punish the children for the sins of their parents to the third and fourth generations. (Exodus 34:7)

*G*od delivered a frightening thought to Moses: The sins of a father could be punished in future generations. Even to this day, children still suffer for the sins of their parents and grandparents. Consider child abuse or alcoholism, for example. While these sins are obvious, sins like selfishness and greed can have long-lasting effects as well. The dire consequences of sin are not limited to individual family members. Be careful not to treat sin casually, but repent and turn from it. Confessing sin may be painful now, but ignoring sin could sting for years to come—in the lives of your descendants.

? Why does God allow innocent children to suffer for the sins of their parents?

? How have you seen the sins of one person affect his or her grandchildren?

? What sins have the most visible consequences in future generations? What less visible sins are just as destructive?

? What can you do to free yourself from sinful patterns your parents may have passed on to you?

? What can you do to guard against passing on some of your own spiritual weaknesses to your children?

COMBINED READINGS

Exodus 35:10—Leviticus 9:6
Matthew 27:32—Mark 4:25
Psalm 34:1–37:29
Proverbs 9:7–10:5

BIBLE MEMORY CHALLENGE

Exodus 40:36-38
Matthew 28:18-20
Psalm 37:23-24
Proverbs 9:11-12

POP QUIZ

OT: What words were engraved on the priests' gold medallion? (Exod. 39:30)

OT: For what purpose did Moses "anoint" Aaron? (Exod. 40:13)

OT: What happened when Moses finished his work of setting up the Tabernacle? (Exod. 40:34-35)

OT: How did the people of Israel know when to move and when to stay? (Exod. 40:36-38)

NT: What happened immediately after Jesus died? (Matt. 27:51-53)

NT: Who met Mary and Mary Magdalene at the tomb early on Sunday morning, and what was his message? (Matt. 28:1-7)

NT: What happened after John baptized Jesus in the Jordan River? (Mark 1:9-11)

NT: How did Jesus respond when the Pharisees criticized him for eating with tax collectors and other sinners? (Mark 2:13-17)

Psalms: How did the psalmist treat his enemies? (35:11-14)

Proverbs: How should we handle a rebuke? (9:7-9)

Just Do It

topic: Devotions

reading: Mark 1:29-45

verse: The next morning Jesus awoke long before daybreak and went out alone into the wilderness to pray.
(Mark 1:35)

*J*esus took time to pray, even though he was the Son of God. In the most demanding years of his ministry, when he served people from early morning until late into the night, he disciplined himself to set apart quiet time to commune with God. Finding time to pray is not easy, but prayer is the vital link between us and God. Like Jesus, we must find time away from others to talk with God, even if we have to get up before daybreak to do it!

? Why do you think Jesus chose to spend so much time in prayer if he was the Son of God?

? Does it make any difference where or when we pray? Why or why not?

? What role should solitude have in the Christian life?

? How is your day different if you start it off in prayer?

? What benefits do you think you would see if you got up earlier to pray?

? What changes can you make in your life that will enable you to spend time in prayer?

COMBINED READINGS

Leviticus 9:7–20:21
Mark 4:26–8:38
Psalm 37:30–42:11
Proverbs 10:6-17

BIBLE MEMORY CHALLENGE

Leviticus 17:11
Mark 8:34-38
Psalm 42:11
Proverbs 10:9

POP QUIZ

OT: How did the people know their sacrifice was accepted? (Lev. 9:23-24)

OT: Why did Nadab and Abihu die? (Lev. 10:1-2)

OT: What is the purpose of a scapegoat? (Lev. 16:7-10)

OT: For what reason should we be holy? (Lev. 19:1-4; 20:7-8)

NT: What surprise did the disciples get in the middle of a fierce storm? (Mark 4:38-41)

NT: What happened when a woman with a hemorrhage touched Jesus' robe? (Mark 5:25-29)

NT: How did the people in Jesus' hometown respond to him and his message? (Mark 6:1-6)

NT: What is the cost of being Jesus' follower, and what is the reward? (Mark 8:34-37)

Psalms: How brief is our time on earth, and why is that important to remember? (39:4-6)

Proverbs: How does love respond when offended? (10:12)

Clean Living

topic: Purity

reading: Leviticus 11:1-47

verse: After all, I, the Lord, am your God. You must be holy because I am holy. So do not defile yourselves by touching any of these animals that scurry along the ground. (Leviticus 11:44)

*T*here is more to this passage than just eating right. These verses provide a key to understanding all the laws and regulations in Leviticus. God wanted his people to be holy, just like himself. His desire hasn't changed. God wants us to be holy, too. Holiness means to be wholly devoted to God. This is no easy task. We find ourselves doing things we know we shouldn't. But as we become more pure and holy, we become more like God.

? Why do people in the world tend to make fun of clean living?

? Why is it so difficult to strive for holiness in today's world?

? Who or what pressures you to conform to impure thinking and living?

? Why does God want you to be pure?

? What do you think it means to be wholly devoted to God?

? What changes could you make in your life to become more pure in God's sight?

COMBINED READINGS

Leviticus 20:22—Numbers 3:51
Mark 9:1–12:17
Psalm 43:1–47:9
Proverbs 10:18-25

BIBLE MEMORY CHALLENGE

Leviticus 20:26
Mark 11:25
Psalm 46:1-2a
Proverbs 10:19

POP QUIZ

OT: Why were priests not allowed to shave their heads or trim their beards? (Lev. 21:5-6)

OT: What is the purpose of the Sabbath? (Lev. 23:1-4)

OT: Why were harvesters told to leave some grain in the field? (Lev. 23:22)

OT: What happened to the man who "blasphemed" the Lord's name? (Lev. 24:10-16, 23)

NT: Why should married couples stay together? (Mark 10:2-9)

NT: What do children have that the rest of us need? (Mark 10:13-15)

NT: What was the rich man unwilling to do to inherit eternal life? (Mark 10:17-22)

NT: Who did the wicked farmers in Jesus' parable represent? (Mark 12:1-12)

Psalms: Why should we not fear, even if the end of the world comes? (46:1-2)

Proverbs: Why should you watch how much you say? (10:19)

Forgive and Be Forgiven

topic: Forgiveness

reading: Mark 11:22-25

verse: When you are praying, first forgive anyone you are holding a grudge against, so that your Father in heaven will forgive your sins, too. (Mark 11:25)

*J*esus gives us a startling warning about forgiveness: If we refuse to forgive others, he will also refuse to forgive us. Why? Because when we don't forgive others, we are denying our condition as sinners in need of God's forgiveness. But when we forgive others, we begin to realize the great debt we as sinners owe to God and that he forgives us out of his great mercy. As we come to understand his mercy, we will want to be like him. Having received forgiveness, we will pass it on to others. Those who are unwilling to forgive have not become one with Christ. It is easy to ask God for forgiveness but difficult to grant it as freely to others.

? When have you struggled to forgive someone? What made the difference in overcoming your struggle, or are you still struggling?

? What sins or offenses by others do you find especially difficult to forgive?

? What prevents you from freely forgiving others?

? What does our unwillingness to forgive others say about us?

? How do you feel when you are holding a grudge against someone? How do you feel when you forgive a person?

? What steps can you take to become more forgiving?

COMBINED READINGS
Numbers 4:1–16:40
Mark 12:18–15:47
Psalm 48:1–54:7
Proverbs 10:26–11:6

BIBLE MEMORY CHALLENGE
Numbers 6:24-26
Mark 14:61-62
Psalm 51:1-13
Proverbs 11:2

POP QUIZ

OT: Who were not allowed to cut their hair, and why? (Num. 6:1-11)

OT: What happened when the people complained? (Num. 11:1-3)

OT: Which two scouts encouraged the Israelites to conquer the Promised Land, and how did God reward them? (Num. 14:6-9, 29-30)

OT: Who was swallowed up by the earth, and why? (Num. 16:1-35)

NT: What are the two most important commandments? (Mark 12:29-31)

NT: Why should we not pay attention to those who say the Messiah is here? (Mark 13:21-22)

NT: Who fell asleep in Gethsemane when Jesus asked them to stay awake? (Mark 14:32-33, 37-41)

NT: Why did Pilate, the Roman governor, have Jesus flogged and crucified? (Mark 15:1-15)

Psalms: When do we become sinners? (51:5)

Proverbs: What guides good and godly people? (11:3, 5)

Apart from God

topic: Loneliness

reading: Mark 15:25-37

verse: Then, at that time Jesus called out with a loud voice, *"Eloi, Eloi, lema sabachthani?"* which means, "My God, my God, why have you forsaken me?" (Mark 15:34)

*J*esus did not ask this question in surprise or despair. He was quoting the first line of Psalm 22. The whole psalm is a prophecy expressing the deep agony of the Messiah's death for the world's sin. Jesus knew this temporary separation from God would come the moment he took upon himself the sins of the world. This separation was what Jesus dreaded as he prayed in Gethsemane. The physical agony was horrible, but the spiritual separation from God was the ultimate pain.

? How has being separated from friends or loved ones caused you to suffer and feel upset?

? When have you felt as if God had deserted you?

? Why is there no loneliness greater than being separated from God?

? To what degree is loneliness a result of spiritual separation?

? In what ways do you attempt to help those who are lonely?

COMBINED READINGS

Numbers 16:41–28:15
Mark 16:1—Luke 3:22
Psalm 55:1–61:8
Proverbs 11:7-17

BIBLE MEMORY CHALLENGE

Numbers 23:19
Luke 1:74-75
Psalm 56:3-4
Proverbs 11:14

POP QUIZ

OT: What happened to Aaron's staff, and why? (Num. 17:1-11)

OT: What did Moses do instead of "commanding" the rock, as God had told him, and what was the result? (Num. 20:7-12)

OT: What did God have Moses do to save the people from the poisonous snakes? (Num. 21:8-9)

OT: Why did Balak want Balaam to come visit? (Num. 22:1-20)

NT: To whom did Jesus first appear after his resurrection? (Mark 16:9)

NT: What were Elizabeth and Zechariah to name their son, and what would he accomplish? (Luke 1:13-17)

NT: What was Mary to name her son, and what would he accomplish? (Luke 1:30-33)

NT: When did Jesus' parents lose track of him, and why? (Luke 2:42-46)

Psalms: Why was David so disturbed by a particular enemy? (55:12-14, 20-21)

Proverbs: What do you receive when you are kind to others? (11:17)

The Great Commission

topic: Witnessing

reading: Mark 16:15-18

verse: Go into all the world and preach the Good News to everyone, everywhere. (Mark 16:15)

*J*esus commanded his disciples to "go into all the world," telling everyone that he had paid the penalty for sin and that those who believe in him would be forgiven and live eternally with God. And, indeed, Christians today are living in all parts of the world, telling this Good News to people who haven't heard it. The driving power that carries missionaries around the world and sets Christ's church in motion is faith in our resurrected Lord. As we grow in our relationship with Christ, he provides us both with opportunities and inner strength to share the Good News.

? Which usually travels faster: good news or bad news?

? How is good news contagious?

? How can you overcome feelings of fear and inadequacy about witnessing to others?

? What would eventually happen if all Christians kept their faith a secret?

? How can you most effectively support missionaries and other Christians who are spreading the good news of Christ?

COMBINED READINGS

Numbers 28:16—Deuteronomy 4:49
Luke 3:23–7:10
Psalm 62:1–68:18
Proverbs 11:18-28

BIBLE MEMORY CHALLENGE

Deuteronomy 4:23-24
Luke 6:31
Psalm 62:6
Proverbs 11:24-25

POP QUIZ

OT: What was not to be done on festival days? (Num. 28:18, 26)

OT: What were the Israelites supposed to do once they arrived in Canaan? (Num. 33:51-56)

OT: What was a city of refuge? (Num. 35:6)

OT: Why is God the only God we should worship? (Deut. 4:32-40)

NT: In what ways did the Devil tempt Jesus in the wilderness? (Luke 4:1-13)

NT: What did Jesus' townspeople try to do to him, and why? (Luke 4:23-30)

NT: How did the paralyzed man get through the crowd to Jesus? (Luke 5:18-19)

NT: Why did Jesus eat with the tax collectors? (Luke 5:31-32)

Psalms: What should be the place of wealth in our life, and why? (62:10-12)

Proverbs: What are the rewards of being generous? (11:25)

Friends and Enemies

topic: Love

reading: Luke 6:27-36

verse: Love your enemies. Do good to those who hate you. Pray for the happiness of those who curse you. Pray for those who hurt you.
(Luke 6:27-28)

*T*he world expects you to show love to your family and friends and expects you to hate your enemies. Christians often adopt the same attitude in many areas of life. But Jesus says we are to love our enemies. If you love your enemies and treat them well, you will truly show that Jesus is the Lord of your life. This is possible only for those who give themselves fully to God, because only he can deliver us from selfishness. We must trust the Holy Spirit to help us love those for whom we may not naturally feel love.

? What television character is most despicable to you? Why?

? Who are your enemies? Why do you love to hate them?

? Have you ever prayed for an enemy? What happened?

? What underlying causes create cliques and unnecessary divisions between groups of people?

? How does a loving spirit demonstrate that we are God's people?

COMBINED READINGS

Deuteronomy 5:1–20:20
Luke 7:11–9:50
Psalm 68:19–73:28
Proverbs 11:29–12:10

BIBLE MEMORY CHALLENGE

Deuteronomy 6:4-6
Luke 9:46-48
Psalm 73:24
Proverbs 11:30

POP QUIZ

OT: What are the Ten Commandments? (Deut. 5:3-21)

OT: What is involved in committing ourselves wholeheartedly to God? (Deut. 6:4-9)

OT: Why did Moses break the two stone tablets of the covenant? (Deut. 9:15-17)

OT: What were the Israelites supposed to destroy when they drove out the Canaanite nations, and why? (Deut. 12:2-4)

NT: What prompted Jesus to forgive the woman who anointed his feet, and how did the men at the table with him respond when he forgave her? (Luke 7:36-50)

NT: Who does Jesus say are his mother and brothers? (Luke 8:19-21)

NT: What did Jesus do with the "Legion" of demons that were in the man from the land of the Gerasenes? (Luke 8:30-33)

NT: Of whom will Jesus be ashamed when he returns in his glory? (Luke 9:26)

Psalms: How often does God carry us in his arms? (68:19)

Proverbs: What kind of people have stability in life? (12:3, 7)

The Fear of God

topic: Reverence

reading:
Deuteronomy 6:20-25

verse: The Lord our God commanded us to obey all these laws and to fear him for our own prosperity and well-being, as is now the case.
(Deuteronomy 6:24)

*T*o reverence God means to fear him. We are accustomed to thinking of fear as a negative emotion. But this passage shows us that fear is necessary in order to obey God. We ought to fear God, or show him the highest reverence, because of the power he has over us. We ought to love God for the mercy he has shown to us. Both fear and love help us to obey.

? What is the difference between being afraid of God and fearing God?

? What are some ways that people demonstrate a lack of fear of (or reverence for) the Lord?

? How does having the "fear of the Lord" help us to become better Christians?

? How can a person develop a proper "fear of the Lord" in his or her life?

? Would you say that your "fear of the Lord" has increased or decreased in the last few years? Explain your answer.

COMBINED READINGS

Deuteronomy 21:1–32:52
Luke 9:51–12:59
Psalm 74:1–78:64
Proverbs 12:11-24

BIBLE MEMORY CHALLENGE

Deuteronomy 30:19-20
Luke 12:27-32
Psalm 74:12
Proverbs 12:24

POP QUIZ

OT: What should you do if you find something that another person has lost? (Deut. 22:1-4)

OT: Why is it important to keep a vow? (Deut. 23:21-23)

OT: How should we provide for the poor, and why? (Deut. 24:17-22)

OT: What encouragement did Moses give Joshua, the new leader? (Deut. 31:7-8)

NT: What did Jesus say about those who look back to earthly things? (Luke 9:62)

NT: How many more messengers did Jesus send out before his death, and why? (Luke 10:1-11)

NT: Why was the Samaritan a "good" neighbor in the parable? (Luke 10:33-35)

NT: Why should we not worry about everyday life? (Luke 12:22-26)

Psalms: How did God provide the thirsty Israelites with water in the wilderness? (78:15-16)

Proverbs: Why should we watch our words? (12:13-14)

Choosing God

topic: Choices

reading:
Deuteronomy 30:11-20

verse: Today I have given you the choice between life and death, between blessings and curses. I call on heaven and earth to witness the choice you make. Oh, that you would choose life, that you and your descendants might live! Choose to love the Lord your God and to obey him and commit yourself to him, for he is your life. Then you will live long in the land the Lord swore to give your ancestors Abraham, Isaac, and Jacob. (Deuteronomy 30:19-20)

*T*he people of Israel had to decide. Would they choose to obey the Lord, who had proven his trustworthiness, or would they choose to obey the local gods, which were man-made idols? Moses challenged them to choose to obey God and therefore continue to experience his blessings. We have to choose who or what we will love and obey: God, our own limited personality, or another imperfect substitute. The right choice brings strength, blessings, and life; the wrong choice results in despair, curses, and death. God first chose us, but he also wants us to choose him. Who will be the master of your life today?

? How do you reconcile the apparent contradiction between God's sovereignty and man's freedom to make choices?

? In what ways does God give you the freedom to choose to follow or reject him?

? When did you choose to follow God? What led you to your decision?

? What area of your life do you hesitate to give completely to the Lord?

? What do you think might happen if you did decide to fully trust God in this area?

COMBINED READINGS
Deuteronomy 33:1—Joshua 12:24
Luke 13:1–17:37
Psalm 78:65–84:12
Proverbs 12:25–13:6

BIBLE MEMORY CHALLENGE
Deuteronomy 33:26-27
Luke 14:26-27
Psalm 79:9
Proverbs 13:3

POP QUIZ

OT: What promise did God give Joshua after Moses' death? (Josh. 1:3-6)

OT: How did Rahab save the two men, and what did they give her in return? (Josh. 2:4-21)

OT: What did the Lord do at the Jordan River to make it possible for Israel to cross? (Josh. 3:14-17)

OT: How many times did the Israelites march around the city of Jericho? (Josh. 6:11-15)

NT: Why was the synagogue leader indignant that Jesus had healed the crippled woman? (Luke 13:14)

NT: Why should we be humble? (Luke 14:8-11)

NT: Whom did Jesus say we should invite to dinner? (Luke 14:12-14)

NT: Why can we not serve both God and money? (Luke 16:13)

Psalms: From where did God call his servant David? (78:70-71)

Proverbs: What is the danger of a quick retort? (13:3)

Returning Thanks

topic: Thankfulness

reading: Luke 17:11-19

verse: He fell face down on the ground at Jesus' feet, thanking him for what he had done. This man was a Samaritan. Jesus asked, "Didn't I heal ten men? Where are the other nine?" (Luke 17:16-17)

*J*esus healed all ten lepers, but only one returned to thank him. It is possible to receive God's great gifts with an ungrateful spirit—nine of the lepers did so. Only the thankful leper, however, learned that his faith played a role in his healing. Likewise, only grateful Christians grow in the understanding of God's grace. God does not demand that we thank him, but he is pleased when we do so, and he uses our spirit of thankfulness to teach us more about his Kingdom.

? Why does God appreciate our thanks?

? What usually inspires or motivates you to express your thanks to the Lord?

? What prevents you from giving thanks to God as much as you should?

? What do you gain when you express your thanks to the Lord?

? For which blessings or in what situations is it difficult for you to say thank you to God?

COMBINED READINGS

Joshua 13:1–24:33
Luke 18:1–21:28
Psalm 85:1–89:52
Proverbs 13:7-23

BIBLE MEMORY CHALLENGE

Joshua 24:14-15
Luke 20:25
Psalm 86:15
Proverbs 13:20

POP QUIZ

OT: How old was Caleb when Moses sent him to explore Canaan? (Josh. 14:6-7)

OT: How could a person escape revenge before a trial? (Josh. 20)

OT: What important reminders did Joshua give the tribes of Reuben, Gad, and the half-tribe of Manasseh? (Josh. 22:4-5)

OT: What would happen if the Israelites disobeyed God? (Josh. 23:15-16)

NT: What did the persistent widow accomplish? (Luke 18:1-5)

NT: Why was the dishonest tax collector justified before God and not the Pharisee? (Luke 18:10-14)

NT: How will Jesus' disciples be repaid for what they give up in this life? (Luke 18:29-30)

NT: If we stand firm even when people hate us because we're Christians, what will we gain? (Luke 21:12-19)

Psalms: What makes God unique from other gods? (86:8-10)

Proverbs: Why should you spend time with wise rather than foolish people? (13:20)

Constant Prayer

topic: Prayer

reading: Luke 18:1-8

verse: One day Jesus told his disciples a story to illustrate their need for constant prayer and to show them that they must never give up.
(Luke 18:1)

*T*o repeat our prayers until the answer comes does not mean endless repetition or painfully long prayer sessions. Constant prayer means keeping our requests continually before God as we live for him day by day, always believing he will answer. Those who live by faith do not easily give up. God may delay answering, but he has good reasons for his delays, and we must never confuse them with neglect. As we persist in prayer, we grow in character, faith, and hope.

? What has been one of your longest running prayer requests with God? What have been the results, if any, so far?

? What benefits have you experienced from continuing in prayer even when no answer seems forthcoming?

? How can you guard against the temptation to give up praying when you do not see immediate results?

? For whom or what would you like to pray every single day?

? What changes can you make in your daily routine to enable you to pray more consistently?

COMBINED READINGS

Judges 1:1–10:18
Luke 21:29–24:53
Psalm 90:1–100:5
Proverbs 13:24–14:12

BIBLE MEMORY CHALLENGE

Judges 5:2
Luke 24:46-48
Psalm 91:1-2
Proverbs 13:24

POP QUIZ

OT: Which tribe was to attack the Canaanites first? (Judg. 1:1-3)

OT: Why did the Israelites begin losing their battles? (Judg. 2:10-23)

OT: Why did God allow godless nations such as the Philistines to remain in the land? (Judg. 3:1-4)

OT: Where was Gideon when the angel of the Lord found him? (Judg. 6:11-12)

NT: Why should we keep a constant watch? (Luke 21:29-36)

NT: What did the bread and wine symbolize at Jesus' last meal with his disciples? (Luke 22:19-20)

NT: Who became friends because of Jesus' arrest? (Luke 23:12)

NT: When did the two traveling to Emmaus recognize Jesus? (Luke 24:28-31)

Psalms: What happens when we make the Lord our refuge? (91:9-10)

Proverbs: What does it prove if you don't discipline your children, and why? (13:24)

Fickle Obedience

topic: Obedience

reading: Judges 2:10-19

verse: Yet Israel did not listen to the judges but prostituted themselves to other gods, bowing down to them. How quickly they turned away from the path of their ancestors, who had walked in obedience to the Lord's commands. (Judges 2:17)

*W*hy would the people of Israel turn so quickly from their faith in God? Simply put, the Canaanite religion appeared more attractive and offered more short-range benefits. One of its most persuasive features was that people could remain selfish and yet fulfill their religious requirements. They could do almost anything they wished and still be obeying at least one of the many Canaanite gods. Sex outside of marriage, for example, was not only allowed but encouraged. True obedience to God means that we will sacrifice our own selfish desires and pledge to do everything God's Word commands.

? For what reasons do whole cultures or societies turn away from God?

? Why do people, sometimes even strong Christians, turn away from obeying God when it is inconvenient?

? Why do you think God was so patient with the people of Israel when they frequently disobeyed him? How has God demonstrated his patience with you?

? What similarities do you see between the Canaanites' religious practices and the practices of our modern-day society?

? How can we better guard against being disobedient to the Lord, as the Israelites were?

? What is an example of an area in which it is inconvenient for you to obey God?

COMBINED READINGS
Judges 11:1—Ruth 4:22
John 1:1–4:54
Psalm 101:1–105:36
Proverbs 14:13-27

BIBLE MEMORY CHALLENGE
Judges 17:6
John 1:12-14
Psalm 102:25-27
Proverbs 14:15-16

POP QUIZ

OT: What did Samson do when a young lion attacked him? (Judg. 14:5-6)

OT: What happened at Samson's wedding party? (Judg. 14:10-20)

OT: What did Ruth do when Naomi urged her to stay in her homeland? (Ruth 1:15-18)

OT: How did God reward Ruth's faithful, hard work? (Ruth 2–4)

NT: What name is given Jesus in the prologue to John's Gospel? (John 1:1-14)

NT: Whom did God send to tell everyone about Jesus? (John 1:6)

NT: What does it mean to become a child of God, and who can do so? (John 1:12-13)

NT: What did Jesus do at a wedding to help the celebration continue, and how did his disciples respond? (John 2:1-11)

Psalms: What good things does God do for us, and what was the psalmist's response? (103:1-5)

Proverbs: Why should we not believe everything we're told? (14:15-16)

Real Worship

topic: Church

reading: John 4:1-26

verse: Believe me, the time is coming when it will no longer matter whether you worship the Father here or in Jerusalem. You Samaritans know so little about the one you worship, while we Jews know all about him, for salvation comes through the Jews. But the time is coming and is already here when true worshipers will worship the Father in spirit and in truth. The Father is looking for anyone who will worship him that way. (John 4:21-23)

*T*he Samaritan woman brought up a popular theological issue—the correct place to worship. However, her question to Jesus about Jerusalem was a smoke screen to cover up her deepest needs. He brought her back to how one should worship and whose help one needs. We are also easily distracted from the main purpose in going to church— to worship the Lord and grow in our knowledge of him. Depend on the Holy Spirit to help you keep your heart and mind focused on God, not earthly matters. Go to church with your heart ready to offer praise to the Lord.

? How are you often distracted from worshiping God when you attend church?

? How can the Holy Spirit help you worship?

? What happens when you don't depend on the Holy Spirit's help?

? How can you tell if your worship is "spiritual and real"?

? How does this passage change your perspective of worship?

? What changes do you need to make to improve your worship?

COMBINED READINGS
1 Samuel 1:1–14:52
John 5:1–7:53
Psalm 105:37–109:31
Proverbs 14:28–15:7

BIBLE MEMORY CHALLENGE
1 Samuel 2:2
John 5:24
Psalm 107:1-3
Proverbs 15:1, 4

POP QUIZ

OT: Why did Peninnah make fun of Hannah? (1 Sam. 1:6)

OT: What happened to Eli's evil sons? (1 Sam. 4:11)

OT: What warning did Samuel give the people about a king, and how did the people respond? (1 Sam. 8:10-20)

OT: What big mistake did Saul make at Gilgal? (1 Sam. 13:7-14)

NT: How did Jesus respond to the Jewish leaders' harassment about breaking the Sabbath? (John 5:16-18)

NT: Why did Jesus withdraw after feeding the immense crowd of over five thousand people? (John 6:15)

NT: Why did Jesus say he is the bread of life? (John 6:33-35)

NT: Why couldn't the people of Jerusalem believe Jesus is the Messiah? (John 7:26-27)

Psalms: If the Lord has saved us, what should we do? (107:2)

Proverbs: What do gentle words accomplish? (15:1, 4)

New Life

topic: Eternal Life

reading: John 5:16-30

verse: I assure you, those who listen to my message and believe in God who sent me have eternal life. They will never be condemned for their sins, but they have already passed from death into life. (John 5:24)

*E*ternal life—living forever with God—begins at conversion. At that moment, new life begins in you. You still face physical death, but when Christ returns again, you will be resurrected to live forever. Have you trusted in Christ and accepted him as your Savior? If you have, you can be confident in his promise of eternal life. As you wait for this great future with your heavenly Father, honor him in all of your actions and attitudes.

? Do you think our enjoyment of eternal life depends upon how we live now? Why or why not?

? If we believers will never be damned for our sins, why should we try to live righteously?

? How did your attitudes and actions change when you became a Christian?

? How can you be confident in your salvation and the promise of eternal life?

? How would your life be different if you were unsure of whether or not you would make it to heaven?

COMBINED READINGS
1 Samuel 15:1–28:25
John 8:1–11:54
Psalm 110:1–117:2
Proverbs 15:8-23

BIBLE MEMORY CHALLENGE
1 Samuel 15:22
John 11:25
Psalm 116:15
Proverbs 15:14

POP QUIZ

OT: How did Saul disobey Samuel's instructions regarding the Amalekites? (1 Sam. 15:1-11)

OT: What did David use to destroy the Philistine champion from Gath? (1 Sam. 17:45-51)

OT: Who made a special vow to be David's friend? (1 Sam. 18:1-3)

OT: How did Abigail save her foolish husband, Nabal, from David's wrath? (1 Sam. 25:18-35)

NT: Why did the adulterous woman's accusers slip away? (John 8:7-9)

NT: Why does Jesus call himself the light of the world? (John 8:12)

NT: How can we know we are truly following Jesus? (John 8:31-32)

NT: When Jesus called himself a gate, what was he saying about his purpose on earth? (John 10:9-10)

Psalms: What is the foundation of true wisdom? (111:10)

Proverbs: What should the wise person be hungry for? (15:14)

True Friends

topic: Friendship

reading: 1 Samuel 23:14-18

verse: So the two of them renewed their covenant of friendship before the Lord. Then Jonathan returned home, while David stayed at Horesh.
(1 Samuel 23:18)

*D*avid was in trouble because King Saul was trying to kill him; so Jonathan risked his life in order to help protect his friend David. One mark of true friendship is being willing to sacrifice your life for your friend. We may not be called upon to risk our life for our friends, but we need to be willing to lay aside our own personal interests in order to help a friend through a trial or difficulty. Think about a few of your friends for a moment. What can you do to help them and to demonstrate your friendship?

? Who was your best friend when you were growing up, and what did you do together?

? Do you tend to have one or two very close friends or several casual friends? Why?

? What do people do formally or informally to establish a pact of friendship?

? What qualities do you look for in a friend?

? What can you change about yourself to become a better friend to the people who are close to you?

COMBINED READINGS
1 Samuel 29:1—2 Samuel 12:31
John 11:55–16:33
Psalm 118:1–119:80
Proverbs 15:24–16:5

BIBLE MEMORY CHALLENGE
2 Samuel 9:8-9, 12-13
John 14:6
Psalm 119:1-3
Proverbs 16:3

POP QUIZ

OT: Why did David kill the Amalekite who said he killed King Saul? (2 Sam. 1:14-16)

OT: What turned Abner from following Saul's dynasty to following David? (2 Sam. 3:6-11)

OT: What kindness did David show Jonathan's crippled son, Mephibosheth? (2 Sam. 9:7-13)

OT: Who confronted David about his sin, and what was the result? (2 Sam. 12:1-23)

NT: Why did Jesus stop his public ministry and leave Jerusalem? (John 11:53-54)

NT: What other person (besides Jesus) did the priests decide to kill to try to stop Jesus' message from spreading? (John 12:10-11)

NT: Why didn't some of the people who believed in Jesus admit it? (John 12:42-43)

NT: Whom did Jesus say he would send to help the disciples—and us? (John 15:26)

Psalms: What is the purpose of God's discipline? (119:67)

Proverbs: How can we be sure our plans will succeed? (16:3)

What Is Truth?

topic: Holy Spirit

reading: John 16:5-15

verse: When the Spirit of truth comes, he will guide you into all truth. He will not be presenting his own ideas; he will be telling you what he has heard. He will tell you about the future.
(John 16:13)

*J*esus promised that the Holy Spirit would tell the disciples about the future—the nature of their mission, the opposition they would face, and the final outcome of their efforts. They didn't fully understand these promises until the Holy Spirit came after Jesus' death and resurrection. Then the Holy Spirit revealed truths to the disciples that they wrote down in the books that compose the New Testament. Not only did God's Spirit help the disciples communicate God's truth to future generations through Scripture, but even today the Holy Spirit helps us understand, interpret, and apply biblical truths to our life.

? Why do unbelievers struggle to understand the Bible?

? How did your understanding of the Bible change after you received God's Spirit?

? What roadblocks hinder you in understanding and applying scriptural truth?

? What biblical truth has the Holy Spirit helped you discover recently?

? How could you rely more on the Holy Spirit to help you get more out of your Bible reading?

COMBINED READINGS

2 Samuel 13:1–21:22
John 17:1—Acts 1:26
Psalm 119:81–121:8
Proverbs 16:6-18

BIBLE MEMORY CHALLENGE

2 Samuel 15:21
Acts 1:8
Psalm 119:105
Proverbs 16:17-18

POP QUIZ

OT: Who conspired to overthrow David? (2 Sam. 15:7-13)

OT: How did David respond when Shimei cursed him and threw stones? (2 Sam. 16:5-13)

OT: How did Absalom get caught when he tried to escape? (2 Sam. 18:9-10)

OT: Who told David to snap out of his grief about Absalom, and why? (2 Sam. 19:5-8)

NT: Why does the world hate those who follow Jesus? (John 17:14)

NT: Why didn't the soldiers break Jesus' legs, as was the custom? (John 19:32-33)

NT: What disciple wouldn't believe until he actually had seen the resurrected Lord? (John 20:24-25)

NT: For whom did Jesus make breakfast after his resurrection? (John 21:1-2, 12-13)

Psalms: From where does our help come? (121:1-8)

Proverbs: What kind of attitude precedes a fall? (16:18)

Hopeful Promises

topic: Hope

reading: Psalm 119:105-117

verse: You are my refuge and my shield; your word is my only source of hope. (Psalm 119:114)

*T*he world around us tells us to seek happiness from a variety of sources: wealth, power, status, friends, even work. In contrast, this psalmist realized that his only hope for happiness and fulfillment was in the Lord. This psalm focuses on the importance of God's Word and how it shows us the best way to live. God's laws are true and wonderful; obedience to them is our only hope, the only way to experience true happiness in this life.

? When have your hopes been dashed? How do you feel about that situation now?

? What kind of hope can the world offer us?

? Where do people who don't trust in Christ look for hope?

? What promise in the Bible has renewed your sense of hope?

? In what area of your life could you depend more on your hope in the Lord and less on artificial substitutes?

COMBINED READINGS
2 Samuel 22:1—1 Kings 7:51
Acts 2:1–7:50
Psalm 122:1–128:6
Proverbs 16:19-33

BIBLE MEMORY CHALLENGE
2 Samuel 22:31-33
Acts 2:38
Psalm 127:1-2
Proverbs 16:24

POP QUIZ

OT: Which of the three punishments from God did David choose, and why? (2 Sam. 24:10-14)

OT: Why did David insist on paying Araunah for his threshing floor and oxen? (2 Sam. 24:21-25)

OT: When God gave Solomon the opportunity to ask for anything, what did Solomon ask for, and why? (1 Kings 3:5-10)

OT: Why could Solomon build the Temple and David could not? (1 Kings 5:3-5)

NT: What happened seven weeks after Jesus' resurrection? (Acts 2:1-4)

NT: What Old Testament prophet predicted Pentecost? (Acts 2:16-21)

NT: How did Peter and John respond when the Jewish council told them not to speak about Jesus? (Acts 4:18-22)

NT: Why did Ananias die? (Acts 5:1-5)

Psalms: What does the Lord think about children? (127:3-5)

Proverbs: How do kind words affect us? (16:24)

Speak Up

topic: Opportunities

reading: Acts 3:12-26

verse: Peter saw his opportunity and addressed the crowd. "People of Israel," he said, "what is so astounding about this? And why look at us as though we had made this man walk by our own power and godliness?" (Acts 3:12)

*P*eter had an audience, and he capitalized on the opportunity to share Jesus Christ. He clearly presented the message of salvation and challenged his listeners to accept God's offer of forgiveness through belief in Jesus Christ. Displays of God's mercy and grace such as the healing of this lame man often create teachable moments. Pray to have courage like Peter to see these opportunities and speak up for Christ.

? Tell about a time that you successfully capitalized on a teachable moment, whether as a volunteer, parent, friend, supervisor, or when witnessing. How did you spot the opportunity?

? Why do you seem to miss so many good opportunities to witness and teach others about Christ?

? What excuses do you give as to why you let so many opportunities to teach and speak up for God slip by?

? In what way is Peter's example inspiring to you?

? What personal fears hinder you from taking advantage of opportunities for God's Kingdom?

? How can you overcome those fears?

COMBINED READINGS
1 Kings 8:1–18:46
Acts 7:51–11:30
Psalm 129:1–135:21
Proverbs 17:1-13

BIBLE MEMORY CHALLENGE
1 Kings 8:57-58
Acts 10:34-35
Psalm 130:3-4
Proverbs 17:3

POP QUIZ

OT: Why did the queen of Sheba visit Solomon, and how did she respond to meeting him? (1 Kings 10:1-10)

OT: How did King Solomon fall into idolatry, and what was the result? (1 Kings 11:1-13)

OT: What did Rehoboam do that caused ten of Israel's tribes to revolt and secede? (1 Kings 12:1-17)

OT: Why did Jeroboam's wife dress up to go see Ahijah? (1 Kings 14:1-6)

NT: Of what did Stephen accuse the Jewish leaders? (Acts 7:51-53)

NT: How did Peter respond when Simon the Sorcerer tried to buy the power of the Holy Spirit from him? (Acts 8:18-23)

NT: How did the believers help Saul escape from the Jewish leaders? (Acts 9:22-25)

NT: What was the significance of Peter's visit to Cornelius's house and the work of the Holy Spirit there? (Acts 11:1-18)

Psalms: What is the problem with earthly idols? (135:15-18)

Proverbs: Those who mock the poor are actually doing what? (17:5)

Feeling like a Failure

topic: Failure

reading: 1 Kings 18:1–19:4

verse: Elijah was afraid and fled for his life. He went to Beersheba, a town in Judah, and he left his servant there. Then he went on alone into the desert, traveling all day. He sat down under a solitary broom tree and prayed that he might die. "I have had enough, Lord," he said. "Take my life, for I am no better than my ancestors." (1 Kings 19:3-4)

*E*lijah felt the depths of fatigue and discouragement just after his two great spiritual victories—the defeat of the prophets of Baal and the answered prayer for rain. Often the feeling of failure sets in after great spiritual experiences, especially those requiring physical effort or producing emotional excitement. To lead him out of depression, God first let Elijah rest and eat. Then God confronted him with the need to return to his mission in life—to be God's prophet. When you feel like a failure, whether or not you deserve to, remember that God still has a purpose for your life.

? Have you ever felt like giving up? What was going on?

? How do you feel after failing at something: depressed, angry, or challenged? Explain your answer.

? When you fail, does this mean you have sinned? Why or why not?

? Why is it easy to feel like a failure even after experiencing a victory?

? How has the Lord comforted you when you have failed?

? How can you comfort another person who feels like a failure?

COMBINED READINGS

1 Kings 19:1—2 Kings 7:20
Acts 12:1–16:15
Psalm 136:1–142:7
Proverbs 17:14-25

BIBLE MEMORY CHALLENGE

2 Kings 7:9
Acts 13:38-39
Psalm 139:1-12
Proverbs 17:14

POP QUIZ

OT: Why did Elijah run for his life? (1 Kings 19:1-3)

OT: What was Elisha doing when Elijah found him? (1 Kings 19:19)

OT: When King Ahab sulked about not getting Naboth's vineyard, what did Jezebel do? (1 Kings 21:7-16)

OT: How was Elijah carried to heaven? (2 Kings 2:11-12)

NT: Who was miraculously released from prison, and why? (Acts 12:1-11)

NT: Why did an angel of the Lord strike Herod with sickness? (Acts 12:22-23)

NT: Why did Paul and Barnabas go to the Gentiles? (Acts 13:46-47)

NT: About what did Paul and Barnabas disagree? (Acts 15:37-40)

Psalms: Why is criticism from godly people helpful? (141:5)

Proverbs: Why should you drop a quarrel? (17:14)

A Secret Strategy

topic: Attitudes

reading: Proverbs 14:30; 15:15; 17:22

verse: A cheerful heart is good medicine, but a broken spirit saps a person's strength. (Proverbs 17:22)

*O*ur attitudes color our whole personality. We cannot always choose what happens to us, but we can choose our attitude toward each situation. The secret to a good attitude is to fill our mind with what is good. Dwelling on the positives in life gives us the proper perspective during hard times. This was Paul's strategy as he faced imprisonment, and it can be ours as we face the struggles of daily living. Look at your attitude, and then examine what you choose to dwell on.

? Tell about a recent day when everything seemed to go wrong. What helped you through that day?

? How does the attitude you adopt first thing in the morning affect the rest of your day?

? How do the books you read, the music you listen to, and the films you watch affect your attitude throughout each day?

? How can a negative attitude be contagious? When has a person's cheerful attitude rubbed off on you?

? When have you made a deliberate choice to have a good attitude in a bad situation? How did your attitude change things?

? What prevents you from dwelling on positive thoughts throughout the day?

COMBINED READINGS

2 Kings 8:1–19:37
Acts 16:16–21:17
Psalm 143:1–149:9
Proverbs 17:26–18:8

BIBLE MEMORY CHALLENGE

2 Kings 17:35-40
Acts 16:31
Psalm 143:10
Proverbs 18:4

POP QUIZ

OT: Who brought Elisha forty camels' worth of products, and why? (2 Kings 8:9)

OT: What instructions did a young prophet give Jehu? (2 Kings 9:6-10)

OT: How was Joash saved from Athaliah's rage? (2 Kings 11:1-3)

OT: Why was King Uzziah struck with leprosy so that he had to live by himself? (2 Kings 15:1-5)

NT: What did the jailer do when he found the prison doors open? (Acts 16:25-34)

NT: How were Paul and Silas released from prison? (Acts 16:35-40)

NT: Where did Paul preach for two years? (Acts 19:9-10)

NT: Why did the believers beg Paul not to go on to Jerusalem? (Acts 21:10-12)

Psalms: What should each generation do? (145:4-7)

Proverbs: What do words of true wisdom accomplish? (18:4)

God Is So Good

topic: Compassion

reading: Psalm 145:1-21

verse: The Lord is good to everyone. He showers compassion on all his creation. (Psalm 145:9)

*L*ife seems unfair to most of us at one time or another. The dishonest are often rewarded, and believers have to endure disappointments, heartaches, and pain. Believers may sometimes wonder whether God is really paying attention or if he truly cares. We can learn from David, the author of this psalm, who trusted in God's great love and compassion even through difficult circumstances. When life seems unfair or God feels far away, focus on his character, compassion, love, and faithfulness. Continue to live the way God wants you to, and trust in his compassion and perfect timing.

? What are some common misconceptions people have about the character of God?

? How do our misconceptions inhibit our ability to trust in God?

? During what time in your life was it difficult for you to trust in God's character and timing?

? Why do you sometimes blame God or distance yourself from him during difficult times?

? Why is it important to focus on God's character when you feel discouraged?

? What can you do to deepen your understanding of God's compassion and love?

COMBINED READINGS
2 Kings 20:1—1 Chronicles 6:81
Acts 21:18–26:32
Psalm 150:1–6:10
Proverbs 18:9-21

BIBLE MEMORY CHALLENGE
1 Chronicles 4:9-10
Acts 22:16
Psalm 5:1-3
Proverbs 18:15

POP QUIZ

OT: How did the Lord prove he would heal Hezekiah? (2 Kings 20:9-10)

OT: How did Josiah respond when Hilkiah the high priest found the Book of the Law and revived the Israelites' interest in it? (2 Kings 22:8–23:28)

OT: For how long was Jerusalem under siege by the Babylonians? (2 Kings 25:1-3)

OT: How did the Babylonian king show kindness to King Jehoiachin? (2 Kings 25:27-30)

NT: What message did Ananias deliver to Paul? (Acts 22:14-15)

NT: Why was the commander frightened that he'd had Paul bound and whipped? (Acts 22:27-29)

NT: What plans did the commander make to ensure Paul's safety? (Acts 23:23-30)

NT: To whom did Paul appeal his case? (Acts 25:11)

Psalms: Why did David experience grief, and how did he deal with it? (6:3-7)

Proverbs: How do intelligent people respond to new ideas? (18:15)

Taking the Plunge

topic: Pride

reading: Proverbs
16:18; 18:12; 29:23

verse: Haughtiness
goes before
destruction; humility
precedes honor.
(Proverbs 18:12)

*T*hose who are proud make the
mistake of underestimating their
weaknesses and discounting potential
stumbling blocks. They sometimes think
they are above the frailties of common
people. With this state of mind they are
easily tripped up. Ironically, proud people
seldom realize that pride is their problem—
although everyone around them is well
aware of it. Ask someone you trust to tell
you whether or not you appear prideful in
any way. This friend may help you avoid
a fall.

? Why does success or fame make one person proud but has
little or no effect on another person?

? How can you tell if a person is prideful?

? How would you approach and confront a fellow Christian
who was caught up in his or her pride?

? How has pride led to destruction in your life?

? Why is a spouse or family member a good person to ask
whether you are proud? What can they tell you that
someone else might not?

? What can you do to avoid becoming proud?

COMBINED READINGS

1 Chronicles 7:1–21:30
Acts 27:1—Romans 3:8
Psalm 7:1–11:7
Proverbs 18:22–19:12

BIBLE MEMORY CHALLENGE

1 Chronicles 16:8-12
Romans 1:16-17
Psalm 8:3-6
Proverbs 19:2

POP QUIZ

OT: Why were the people of Judah exiled to Babylon? (1 Chron. 9:1)

OT: For what reasons did Saul die? (1 Chron. 10:13-14)

OT: Whom did David choose to be commander of his bodyguard? (1 Chron. 11:24-25)

OT: Why did Uzzah die while moving the Ark? (1 Chron. 13:9-10)

NT: What did Paul tell the ship's crew in the middle of the storm to encourage them? (Acts 27:22-24)

NT: Whom did Paul heal on Malta, and what was the result? (Acts 28:7-10)

NT: Why was Paul not ashamed of the Good News? (Rom. 1:16-17)

NT: Why did God abandon men to shameful desires? (Rom. 1:21-25)

Psalms: What is the position and responsibility of human beings in God's created order? (8:4-8)

Proverbs: Why should we think before acting? (19:2)

God's Patience

topic: Patience

reading: Romans 2:1-11

verse: Don't you realize how kind, tolerant, and patient God is with you? Or don't you care? Can't you see how kind he has been in giving you time to turn from your sin? (Romans 2:4)

*W*e can easily mistake God's patience for approval of the wrong way we are living. Self-evaluation is difficult, and it is even more difficult to expose our life to God and let him tell us where we need to change. But as Christians we must pray constantly that God will point out our sins so that he can deliver us from them. We should be grateful for his patience toward us. Unfortunately, we are more likely to be amazed at God's patience with others than we are to be humbled at his patience with us.

? How does God demonstrate his patience with us?

? Why is God so patient with us?

? Why do we tend to mistake God's patience for approval?

? Why do people often wait for God's obvious disapproval and discipline before changing their ways?

? For what reasons can you thank God for his patience in your life?

COMBINED READINGS
1 Chronicles 22:1—2 Chronicles 8:10
Romans 3:9–8:8
Psalm 12:1–18:15
Proverbs 19:13-25

BIBLE MEMORY CHALLENGE
2 Chronicles 7:14
Romans 3:23-24
Psalm 15:1-5
Proverbs 19:20-21

POP QUIZ

OT: Who began planning the construction of the Temple? (1 Chron. 22:5; 28:11-19)

OT: What did Solomon have more of than any other king before or since? (2 Chron. 1:12)

OT: When and where did construction begin on the Temple? (2 Chron. 3:1-2)

OT: Why did David want to build the Temple? (2 Chron. 6:7-11)

NT: How are we made right in God's sight? (Rom. 3:22-25)

NT: How is Abraham the father of all who believe? (Rom. 4:16-24)

NT: Why was God's law given? (Rom. 5:20-21)

NT: Why should we not let sin control us? (Rom. 6:12-14)

Psalms: What kinds of people say there is no God, and what is the result? (14:1-3)

Proverbs: What makes a person truly attractive? (19:22)

Getting Humble

topic: Humility

reading: 2 Chronicles 7:11-22

verse: If my people who are called by my name will humble themselves and pray and seek my face and turn from their wicked ways, I will hear from heaven and will forgive their sins and heal their land.
(2 Chronicles 7:14)

*S*olomon asked God to make provisions for the people when they sinned. God answered with four conditions for forgiveness: (1) Humble yourself by admitting your sins; (2) pray to God for forgiveness; (3) search for God continually; (4) and turn from sinful habits. The first step to true repentance is humility. If we proudly excuse or rationalize our sin, we distance ourselves from the Lord. Have you ever felt like your prayers were bouncing off the ceiling? Check your attitudes and your actions; a prayer of repentance may open the lines of communication between you and God.

? When have you felt a communication barrier between you and the Lord? What did you do?

? Why is humility a necessary ingredient for true repentance?

? What value does our world place on humility? How is God's view different?

? How have you seen humility benefit your relationship with another person?

? How have you seen humility benefit your relationship with God?

? What can you do to better cultivate a spirit of humility?

COMBINED READINGS

2 Chronicles 8:11–25:28
Romans 8:9–12:21
Psalm 18:16–22:31
Proverbs 19:26–20:10

BIBLE MEMORY CHALLENGE

2 Chronicles 16:9a
Romans 10:9-11
Psalm 19:14
Proverbs 20:3

POP QUIZ

OT: Why was there peace during Asa's reign? (2 Chron. 14:2-7)

OT: Why did King Asa depose his grandmother from her position as queen mother? (2 Chron. 15:16)

OT: Who was so wicked that nobody was sorry when he died? (2 Chron. 21:20)

OT: What king threatened a prophet with death if he didn't be quiet? (2 Chron. 25:14-16)

NT: What inheritance do we receive as God's children? (Rom. 8:16-17)

NT: Why shouldn't we criticize God and his actions? (9:20-24)

NT: From what does salvation come? (Rom. 10:8-10)

NT: What can we do that will help us to know God's will? (Rom. 12:1-2)

Psalms: Why are the laws of the Lord so important? (19:7-11)

Proverbs: Why should we avoid fights? (20:3)

Honest with Yourself

topic: Honesty

reading: Romans 12:3-8

verse: As God's messenger, I give each of you this warning: Be honest in your estimate of yourselves, measuring your value by how much faith God has given you. (Romans 12:3)

*W*e hear a lot about the importance of healthy self-esteem. Paul warns us, however, not to go too far in self-love. No one should think of himself more highly than he ought. Some think too little of themselves; some think too much of themselves. The key to an honest and accurate evaluation is knowing the basis of our self-worth—our new identity in Christ. Evaluating yourself by the worldly standards of success and achievement can cause you to think either too much or too little about your worth in the eyes of others and miss your true value in God's eyes.

? When talking about themselves, why do some people embellish the facts to make themselves look better?

? Is it possible to "like yourself" when you know that you are a sinner? Explain your reasoning.

? Identify some events in your life that have developed or hindered your own sense of self-worth. How did Christ change that?

? How does being a Christian affect the way you feel about yourself?

? How can you become more honest in your estimate of yourself?

COMBINED READINGS

2 Chronicles 26:1—Ezra 2:70
Romans 13:1—1 Corinthians 2:5
Psalm 23:1–27:14
Proverbs 20:11-23

BIBLE MEMORY CHALLENGE

2 Chronicles 26:16a
Romans 13:12
Psalm 24:3-6
Proverbs 20:13

POP QUIZ

OT: What happened as a result of Ahaz's godlessness as a king? (2 Chron. 28:4-8)

OT: Who repaired the doors of the Temple? (2 Chron. 29:3)

OT: Why was King Hezekiah so highly respected among the surrounding nations? (2 Chron. 32:20-23)

OT: Who allowed the people to return to Jerusalem to rebuild the Temple? (Ezra 1:1-4)

NT: Why should we obey the government? (Rom. 13:1-5)

NT: How did Paul win over the Gentiles? (Rom. 15:18-19)

NT: What reason did Paul give for Christians to avoid divisions and to live in harmony? (1 Cor. 1:10-13)

NT: Why did Paul focus on Jesus Christ and his death on the cross? (1 Cor. 2:1-5)

Psalms: Why should we not be afraid of death? (23:4)

Proverbs: Why should you not love sleep? (20:13)

Values Clash

topic: Values

reading: Romans 14:1-23

verse: Those who think it is all right to eat anything must not look down on those who won't. And those who won't eat certain foods must not condemn those who do, for God has accepted them. (Romans 14:3)

*I*t is very easy to judge and criticize other believers for having different values and priorities than we do. However, this passage clearly teaches that each person is ultimately accountable to Christ, not to others. While we should be uncompromising in our stand against activities expressly forbidden by Scripture, we should be careful to avoid condemning others for activities that simply oppose our personal preferences. Instead of focusing on our differences, we should focus on our common desire to honor Christ.

? What are some potentially divisive differences in values you have observed in your church or among your friends?

? What are some values Christians hold as personal convictions that are not clearly supported by Scripture?

? What are some of the benefits of having differing values and priorities represented within a church body?

? How can differences of opinion easily separate and destroy the body of Christ?

? How can we hold each other accountable to Christian standards without being critical about an inconsequential difference in values?

? In what area do you need to be careful about wrongly condemning others?

COMBINED READINGS

Ezra 3:1—Nehemiah 5:13
1 Corinthians 2:6–7:40
Psalm 28:1–32:11
Proverbs 20:24–21:7

BIBLE MEMORY CHALLENGE

Nehemiah 1:5-6
1 Corinthians 6:14
Psalm 32:1-2
Proverbs 21:5-6

POP QUIZ

OT: What did the Israelites who had returned from Babylon do, even though they were afraid of the local residents? (Ezra 3:3)

OT: Why did the older people weep when they saw the new Temple's foundation? (Ezra 3:12-13)

OT: When Ezra discovered the Israelites had intermarried with pagan women, what did he do? (Ezra 9:3; 10:1)

OT: Who were the Israelites' two worst enemies while building the Temple? (Neh. 4:1-3)

NT: How can we understand spiritual things? (1 Cor. 2:10-15)

NT: How does Paul indict the Corinthians about their quarreling? (1 Cor. 3:1-4)

NT: What kinds of people will have no part in the Kingdom of God? (1 Cor. 6:9-10)

NT: What kind of sin affects your body the most? (1 Cor. 6:18-20)

Psalms: What did David ask God to do with the wicked? (28:3-4)

Proverbs: What leads to prosperity, and what leads to poverty? (21:5)

Realistic Expectations

topic: Marriage

reading:
1 Corinthians 7:25-40

verse: But if you do get married, it is not a sin. And if a young woman gets married, it is not a sin. However, I am trying to spare you the extra problems that come with marriage. (1 Corinthians 7:28)

*M*any people naively think that marriage will solve all their problems. Here are some problems that marriage won't solve: loneliness, sexual temptation, satisfaction of one's deepest emotional needs, and elimination of life's difficulties. Marriage alone does not hold two people together but commitment does—commitment to Christ and to each other despite conflicts and problems. Whether married or single, we must be content with our situation and focus on Christ, not on other people, to solve our problems.

? What are some of the pros and cons of the single life?

? What are the pros and cons of married life?

? What unrealistic expectations do young people tend to have about marriage?

? What are some wrong reasons for getting married? What are some wrong reasons to remain single?

? What couple that you know displays several ingredients of a good marriage?

? In what area of your life do you need to rely more on Christ to solve your problems instead of depending on your spouse or friends?

COMBINED READINGS

Nehemiah 5:14—Esther 7:10
1 Corinthians 8:1–12:26
Psalm 33:1–36:12
Proverbs 21:8-22

BIBLE MEMORY CHALLENGE

Nehemiah 9:6
1 Corinthians 10:13
Psalm 34:6-9
Proverbs 21:21

POP QUIZ

OT: Why did Nehemiah refuse to claim the governor's food allowance? (Neh. 5:18-19)

OT: What happened when Queen Vashti refused to appear before King Xerxes' company? (Esther 1:10-22)

OT: For what reason did Haman decide to destroy all the Jews? (Esther 3:5-6)

OT: What did Mordecai encourage Esther to do, even though it was dangerous? (Esther 4:13-16)

NT: Why do we have to be careful what we do as Christians? (1 Cor. 8:9)

NT: How should we handle temptations? (1 Cor. 10:13)

NT: Why should we examine ourselves before participating in the Lord's Supper? (1 Cor. 11:27-29)

NT: Why is each spiritual gift important? (1 Cor. 12:12-26)

Psalms: How did God create the world, according to the psalmist? (33:6)

Proverbs: What causes joy to the godly but dismay to the wicked? (21:15)

Resistible Temptation

topic: Temptation

reading:
1 Corinthians 10:1-13

verse: Remember that the temptations that come into your life are no different from what others experience. And God is faithful. He will keep the temptation from becoming so strong that you can't stand up against it. When you are tempted, he will show you a way out so that you will not give in to it.
(1 Corinthians 10:13)

*I*n a culture filled with moral depravity and pressures, Paul gave strong encouragement to the Corinthians about temptation. God will help us resist temptation, but it is our responsibility to resist the temptation when it occurs. Like a commander of an army, God will supply his troops with the weapons they need to win the battle. However, as the Lord's foot soldiers, we must be ready and willing to pick up our weapons and fight. Temptation will only defeat us when we do not trust in the Lord for his guidance and strength.

? What temptations are commonly considered irresistible?

? How can resisting temptation sometimes incur the scorn of the world?

? How has the Lord provided a means of escape for you during times of temptation?

? What weapons has the Lord provided for his children to fight against temptation? Which has proven to be especially useful for you?

? What can you do to strengthen yourself in an area where you have fallen to temptation?

COMBINED READINGS

Esther 8:1—Job 22:30
1 Corinthians 12:27—
  2 Corinthians 1:11
Psalm 37:1–40:17
Proverbs 21:23–22:4

BIBLE MEMORY CHALLENGE

Job 1:21
1 Corinthians 15:3-4
Psalm 37:3-4
Proverbs 22:1-4

POP QUIZ

OT: How did the king's decree (dictated by Mordecai) protect the Jews? (Esther 8:11-14)

OT: What did Job do after his children's birthday celebrations? (Job 1:4-5)

OT: How did Job respond to losing everything? (Job 1:20-22)

OT: Why did God allow Satan to further inflict trouble on Job? (Job 2:3-7)

NT: What three things will endure for all time? (1 Cor. 13:13)

NT: What should be our highest goal as Christians? (1 Cor. 14:1)

NT: Why is Christ's resurrection from the dead so important to our faith? (1 Cor. 15:30-32)

NT: What happens when we suffer for Christ? (2 Cor. 1:5-6)

Psalms: Why shouldn't we envy those who look and act "successful"? (37:1-2, 8-10)

Proverbs: What do the rich and the poor have in common? (22:2)

A Secure Investment

topic: Heaven

reading: Job 22:21-30

verse: Give up your lust for money, and throw your precious gold into the river. Then the Almighty himself will be your treasure. He will be your precious silver! (Job 22:24-25)

*E*liphaz reminded Job of the importance of desiring eternal treasure. Jesus says, "Sell what you have and give to those in need. This will store up treasure for you in heaven! . . . Your treasure will be safe—no thief can steal it and no moth can destroy it" (Luke 12:33). Money, gold, and other material possessions are only temporary, and our first priority in life should not be to accumulate earthly wealth. But God will last forever, and a personal relationship with him should be our first and most precious treasure.

? What possessions do you treasure most and why?

? How can you keep from becoming too attached to your earthly possessions?

? Do you think some people will have more treasures in heaven than others? Why or why not?

? In addition to giving to the needy, how else can you store up treasure in heaven?

? How can you treasure your relationship with Jesus more than your possessions?

COMBINED READINGS
Job 23:1—Ecclesiastes 3:22
2 Corinthians 1:12–6:13
Psalm 41:1–46:11
Proverbs 22:5-15

BIBLE MEMORY CHALLENGE
Job 42:1-6
2 Corinthians 5:10
Psalm 42:1
Proverbs 22:7

POP QUIZ

OT: Why is wisdom so rare, and where can it be found? (Job 28:12-28)

OT: How did Job respond when God confronted him? (42:1-6)

OT: In what ways did the Lord bless Job after testing him? (Job 42:10-17)

OT: How did the Teacher try to find meaning in his life? (Eccles. 2:1-11)

NT: How does God identify us as his own? (2 Cor. 1:21-22)

NT: Where does our power and success come from? (2 Cor. 3:5-6)

NT: When troubles come, how can we gain a right perspective? (2 Cor. 4:17-18)

NT: What should our aim in life be? (2 Cor. 5:9-10)

Psalms: What reward does the Lord give those who are kind to the poor? (41:1-3)

Proverbs: Why should you be careful from whom you borrow money? (22:7)

Never Give Up

topic: Quitting

reading:
2 Corinthians 4:8-18

verse: We are pressed on every side by troubles, but we are not crushed and broken. We are perplexed, but we don't give up and quit.
(2 Corinthians 4:8)

*P*aul reminds us that though we may be at the end of our rope, we are never at the end of our hope. Our perishable bodies are subject to sin and suffering, but God never abandons us. Because Christ won victory over death, we have eternal life. All our risks, humiliations, and trials are opportunities to demonstrate Christ's power and presence in us. As Christians, we are never to give up because God is not finished ministering through us.

? When have you recently felt like quitting? Why did you stop, or what kept you going?

? Over what in life do you most often become discouraged? Why?

? How does refusing to give up demonstrate Christ's power and presence in us?

? How has God kept you going through a difficult time?

? When you feel like quitting, to whom do you talk in order to gain encouragement? Why do you go to this person?

? In what aspect of your faith do you need to redouble your efforts?

COMBINED READINGS

Ecclesiastes 4:1—Isaiah 5:30
2 Corinthians 6:14—11:15
Psalm 47:1–53:6
Proverbs 22:16-29

BIBLE MEMORY CHALLENGE

Ecclesiastes 12:13-14
2 Corinthians 9:7
Psalm 49:16-17
Proverbs 22:17-18

POP QUIZ

OT: What are the benefits of working together? (Eccles. 4:9-12)

OT: What is the wise king's final conclusion? (Eccles. 12:13-14)

OT: What happened in the young woman's dream when she hesitated to let her lover in? (Song 5:2-8)

OT: What did God want his people to do instead of offering ritual prayers? (Isa. 1:14-17)

NT: Why should we not team up with unbelievers? (2 Cor. 6:14-18)

NT: How can God use sorrow in our life? (2 Cor. 7:10-11)

NT: What happens when you give generously? (2 Cor. 9:8-14)

NT: How can we, as humans, wage war against the Devil? (2 Cor. 10:3-5)

Psalms: How much does it cost to have eternal life? (49:8-10)

Proverbs: Why should you steer clear of angry people? (22:24-25)

Lifetime Goals

topic: Goals

reading: Ecclesiastes 12:13-14

verse: Here is my final conclusion: Fear God and obey his commands, for this is the duty of every person. (Ecclesiastes 12:13)

*I*n Ecclesiastes Solomon shows us that we should enjoy life, but this does not exempt us from obeying God's commands. We should search for purpose and meaning in life. But this does not come by immersing ourselves in the pleasures of this world. We need to acknowledge the evil, foolishness, and injustice in life, yet maintain a positive attitude and strong faith in God. The goal of fearing God and doing what he commands should encompass everything we do.

? Do you think it is important to have specific, written, lifetime goals? Why or why not?

? With what sorts of pursuits do people try to fill the emptiness in their lives?

? What is your favorite pastime, recreation, or hobby? Why do you enjoy doing it?

? How should a Christian's view of success differ from our society's view of success?

? What does it mean to fear the Lord? How does it make a difference in your day-to-day activities?

COMBINED READINGS
Isaiah 6:1–24:23
2 Corinthians 11:16—Galatians 3:9
Psalm 54:1–60:12
Proverbs 23:1-16

BIBLE MEMORY CHALLENGE
Isaiah 9:6-7
Galatians 2:19-21
Psalm 57:9-11
Proverbs 23:4-5

POP QUIZ

OT: How did Isaiah respond to seeing the Lord? (Isa. 6:1-5)

OT: What sign did Isaiah give Ahaz that was also a prophecy about Jesus? (Isa. 7:14-15)

OT: What were the royal titles for the child who would be born to save the world? (Isa. 9:6)

OT: Why did Isaiah walk around naked and barefoot for three years? (Isa. 20:1-4)

NT: What hardships did Paul suffer for Christ? (2 Cor. 11:23-27)

NT: What did Paul receive to keep him from becoming proud, and why was that a danger? (2 Cor. 12:6-7)

NT: How can we know if our faith is genuine? (2 Cor. 13:3-6)

NT: Why did Paul publicly confront Peter? (Gal. 2:11-16)

Psalms: How often did the psalmist plead with God to rescue him? (55:16-17)

Proverbs: Why is trying to get rich a waste of time? (23:4-5)

The Prince of Peace

topic: Peace

reading: Isaiah 9:6-7

verse: For a child is born to us, a son is given to us. And the government will rest on his shoulders. These will be his royal titles: Wonderful Counselor, Mighty God, Everlasting Father, Prince of Peace. His ever expanding, peaceful government will never end. He will rule forever with fairness and justice from the throne of his ancestor David. The passionate commitment of the Lord Almighty will guarantee this! (Isaiah 9:6-7)

*I*saiah's prophecy promised a Messiah who would bring peace and justice to a world ravaged by hatred and suffering. This message of hope was fulfilled in the birth of Christ and the establishment of his eternal Kingdom. He came to deliver all people from their slavery to sin. If we choose to accept his forgiveness, we can experience the great joy and peace that comes from a relationship with our heavenly Father.

? Why is Jesus called the "Prince of Peace"?

? When did you first experience a sense of God's peace?

? What responsibility do Christians have to promote peace in their communities?

? How can Christians bring peace to a fallen world torn by injustice?

? In what area of your life do you want to experience God's peace more completely?

COMBINED READINGS
Isaiah 25:1–43:13
Galatians 3:10—Ephesians 2:22
Psalm 61:1–67:7
Proverbs 23:17-35

BIBLE MEMORY CHALLENGE
Isaiah 40:27-31
Ephesians 2:8-10
Psalm 63:1-5
Proverbs 23:17-18

POP QUIZ

OT: What happens to those who try to hide their plans from God? (Isa. 29:15-16)

OT: What would finally destroy Assyria? (Isa. 31:8-9)

OT: What is the Highway of Holiness, and where does it lead? (Isa. 35:8-10)

OT: Why did God send Hezekiah's sickness? (Isa. 38:15-17)

NT: How can a person be made right with God? (Gal. 3:10-14)

NT: Why can we call the almighty God "Father"? (Gal. 4:4-7)

NT: What kind of freedom does the Christian have? (Gal. 5:13-14)

NT: How has Christ himself made peace between the Jews and Gentiles? (Eph. 2:14-18)

Psalms: Who will find shelter in the Lord? (64:10)

Proverbs: Who has anguish and sorrow, and why? (23:29-35)

Confidence Is Your Strength

topic: Confidence

reading: Isaiah 30:15-17

verse: The Sovereign Lord, the Holy One of Israel, says, "Only in returning to me and waiting for me will you be saved. In quietness and confidence is your strength. But you would have none of it."
(Isaiah 30:15)

*D*oes this verse sound like your life? Like the Hebrew people, we often refuse to wait upon the Lord and trust confidently in him. When faced with a question or problem in life, there is nothing wrong with waiting. In fact, if we are confident that we are living righteously for the Lord, the best thing for us to do is wait. Unfortunately, this is often the most difficult thing to do. Sometimes, from our perspective, God does not move fast enough. This is why confidence is so important. By trusting and believing that the Lord will take care of us, we can gain the patience necessary to wait upon him.

? What has been an issue in your life in which you found it difficult to wait for the Lord to give an answer?

? Think back to an Old Testament example of when someone did not wait confidently in the Lord. What parallels can you see in your own life?

? When you're faced with a problem, to whom do you turn for advice? What does he or she usually say that helps you?

? Who is someone you know who has a lot of confidence in the Lord? How did this person build his or her confidence in God?

? What is something you can do this week to strengthen your own confidence in God?

COMBINED READINGS
Isaiah 43:14–62:5
Ephesians 3:1—Philippians 2:18
Psalm 68:1–72:20
Proverbs 24:1-12

BIBLE MEMORY CHALLENGE
Isaiah 55:6
Philippians 2:3-11
Psalm 68:19-20
Proverbs 24:11-12

POP QUIZ

OT: Why did God consider Babylon to be so wicked? (Isa. 47:8-11)

OT: What steps could the Israelites take to turn from their sins? (Isa. 55:6-7)

OT: Why was it hard for the Israelites to understand God? (Isa. 55:8-9)

OT: Why can't we hear God sometimes? (Isa. 59:1-3)

NT: How can we lead a life worthy of our calling by God? (Eph. 4:1-3)

NT: What happens when a godly person "shines" his light in a dark place? (Eph. 5:13-14)

NT: Why should we do our work enthusiastically? (Eph. 6:7-8)

NT: What kind of attitude should we have? (Phil. 2:5-7)

Psalms: How does God help the lonely? (68:5-6)

Proverbs: Why should we be responsible for others? (24:11-12)

Sunburned Soul

topic: Anger

reading: Ephesians 4:17-32

verse: And "don't sin by letting anger gain control over you." Don't let the sun go down while you are still angry. (Ephesians 4:26)

*T*he Bible doesn't tell us we should never feel angry, but it points out that it is important to handle our anger properly. If ventilated thoughtlessly, anger can hurt others and destroy relationships. If bottled up inside, it can cause us to become bitter and can destroy our mental, physical, and spiritual health from within. Paul tells us to deal with our anger immediately in a way that rebuilds relationships instead of destroying them. If we nurse our anger, we give Satan a foothold in our life.

? Why does it feel so good to "nurse a grudge"?

? What happens when you let the sun go down on your anger?

? Why do we hesitate to resolve our differences with others quickly?

? Why does it get more difficult to reconcile with others the longer you wait?

? What ought to happen when anger separates fellow believers in the church?

? With whom are you somewhat angry right now? How can you begin to resolve your differences with that person before the sun goes down today?

COMBINED READINGS
Isaiah 62:6—Jeremiah 9:26
Philippians 2:19—Colossians 3:17
Psalm 73:1–78:55
Proverbs 24:13-27

BIBLE MEMORY CHALLENGE
Isaiah 64:6
Colossians 1:15-17
Psalm 73:25-26
Proverbs 24:13-14

POP QUIZ

OT: Whom did Isaiah see marching in red-stained clothing from Edom, and why were they marching? (Isa. 63:1-6)

OT: What was Jeremiah's excuse for not speaking out for God, and how did God answer? (Jer. 1:4-8)

OT: What did God tell Israel they must do to stay in the land? (Jer. 7:1-7)

OT: What did God promise to do to his people who were liars? (Jer. 9:3-9)

NT: What does Paul consider to be worthless, and why? (Phil. 3:4-9)

NT: Why should we not worry? (Phil. 4:6-7)

NT: What is involved in living in obedience to Christ? (Col. 2:6-10)

NT: What should we set our sights on, and why? (Col. 3:1-4)

Psalms: Why is it important to learn from the past? (78:1-8)

Proverbs: Why shouldn't we associate with rebels? (24:21-22)

Choose to Pray

topic: Worry

reading: Philippians 4:1-9

verse: Don't worry about anything; instead, pray about everything. Tell God what you need, and thank him for all he has done. (Philippians 4:6)

*I*t often seems easier to worry about our problems than to trust God with them. However, Paul advises us to pray about everything, instead of worrying. This takes our focus off of our inability to solve our problems and turns our eyes to Christ, who can meet our needs beyond our wildest expectations. Turn to God in prayer each time you are tempted to worry about something, and he will bless you with overwhelming peace. In reality, it is much easier to trust God than to worry!

? Is there anything in life we should worry about?

? What is the difference between having concerns and worrying?

? How can prayer be used as an effective weapon against worrying?

? If you worried less, how do you think your family and personal life would be affected?

? What steps can you take now to reduce your level of anxiety?

COMBINED READINGS
Jeremiah 10:1–25:38
Colossians 3:18—
  2 Thessalonians 2:17
Psalm 78:56–84:12
Proverbs 24:28–25:15

BIBLE MEMORY CHALLENGE
Jeremiah 15:16
1 Thessalonians 5:16-18
Psalm 84:10-12
Proverbs 25:15

POP QUIZ

OT: What's the difference between the God of Israel and other gods? (Jer. 10:11-16)

OT: What will happen to any nation that refuses to obey God? (Jer. 12:17)

OT: What message did God give Israel through Jeremiah's linen belt? (Jer. 13:1-11)

OT: What happened to Judah when God held back the rain? (Jer. 14:1-7)

NT: How should we act around unbelievers? (Col. 4:5-6)

NT: Why was Paul thankful for the Thessalonian believers? (1 Thess. 1:2-3; 2 Thess. 1:3-4)

NT: What will happen when the Lord returns? (1 Thess. 4:13–5:3)

NT: Why should we not be shaken by those who claim that the day of the Lord has already begun? (2 Thess. 2:1-6)

Psalms: Why should God help Israel, according to Asaph? (79:9)

Proverbs: What is the result of sleeping too much? (24:32-34)

Gentleness

topic: Caring

reading:
1 Thessalonians
2:1-20

verse: As apostles of Christ we certainly had a right to make some demands of you, but we were as gentle among you as a mother feeding and caring for her own children.
(1 Thessalonians 2:7)

*P*aul demonstrated gentleness in his ministry to the Thessalonians. Gentleness is not a very highly respected quality in our world. Power and assertiveness gain more respect, even though none of us likes to be bullied. Gentleness is love in action—being considerate, caring for the needs of others, allowing time for the other person to talk, and being willing to learn. It is an essential trait for Christian men and women. To follow Christ's example, we should care for the needs of others with a gentle and loving spirit.

? Does gentleness help you get ahead in life? Why or why not?

? What do you think are the likely results of Christians who help others without a spirit of gentleness?

? In what situations are you too gentle? In what situations do you need to be more gentle?

? How do Christians learn what it means to be gentle?

? How can you be more like Christ in the way you care for others?

COMBINED READINGS
Jeremiah 26:1–38:28
2 Thessalonians 3:1—1 Timothy 6:21
Psalm 85:1–89:52
Proverbs 25:16-28

BIBLE MEMORY CHALLENGE
Jeremiah 29:11
1 Timothy 6:6-10
Psalm 86:11
Proverbs 25:21-22

POP QUIZ

OT: What did the yoke that Jeremiah wore symbolize? (Jer. 27:2-8)

OT: When Hananiah removed Jeremiah's yoke, what happened? (Jer. 28:10-17)

OT: How long did Jeremiah predict the Israelites would be in Babylon? (Jer. 29:10)

OT: What would happen when God made a "new covenant" with Israel? (Jer. 31:33-34)

NT: Why should we work hard and stay away from lazy Christians? (2 Thess. 3:6-15)

NT: Why did Paul urge Timothy to stay in Ephesus? (1 Tim. 1:3-5)

NT: Why is spiritual exercise more important than physical exercise? (1 Tim. 4:8)

NT: Why is the love of money at the root of all kinds of evil? (1 Tim. 6:9-10)

Psalms: What reasons did David give for God to help and save him? (86:1-4)

Proverbs: How should we treat our enemies, and why? (25:21-22)

Caring for Your Own

topic: Family

reading: 1 Timothy 5:1-25

verse: Those who won't care for their own relatives, especially those living in the same household, have denied what we believe. Such people are worse than unbelievers. (1 Timothy 5:8)

*A*lmost everyone has relatives—or extended family of some kind. Family relationships are so important in God's eyes, Paul says that a person who neglects his family responsibilities is denying the faith. Family should be an important value of all believers.

? How close is your extended family? How do you keep in touch with them?

? Why is a person who neglects the needs of his relatives denying "what we believe"?

? What impression do you think unbelievers get when they see believers neglect the needs of their own families?

? How do we care properly for needy family members without enabling them in unhealthy ways?

? What prevents you from helping family members as much as you would like to or think you should?

? Which of your family members most need your attention or active care? How can you best help them?

COMBINED READINGS

Jeremiah 39:1–52:34
2 Timothy 1:1—Titus 3:15
Psalm 90:1–100:5
Proverbs 26:1-19

BIBLE MEMORY CHALLENGE

Jeremiah 46:27-28
2 Timothy 3:16-17
Psalm 91:14-16
Proverbs 26:18-19

POP QUIZ

OT: What proof did the Lord offer to the Israelites that they would be punished in Egypt? (Jer. 44:29-30)

OT: Which area was known for its medicines and healing? (Jer. 46:11)

OT: Why did God judge Moab? (Jer. 48:35)

OT: The world will be shocked when which city falls? (Jer. 51:41)

NT: Why was Paul willing to endure hardship? (2 Tim. 2:10)

NT: Why is purity so important? (2 Tim. 2:21)

NT: What are the source and the purpose of the Bible? (2 Tim. 3:16-17)

NT: Why is right living so important? (Titus 2:6-8)

Psalms: Why should we make the best of our time? (90:9-12)

Proverbs: How bad is it to lie to a friend? (26:18-19)

Where to Turn for Help

topic: Bible

reading: 2 Timothy 3:14-17

verse: All Scripture is inspired by God and is useful to teach us what is true and to make us realize what is wrong in our lives. It straightens us out and teaches us to do what is right. (2 Timothy 3:16)

*W*hat is the meaning of life? Why am I here? Does anybody care? We sometimes ask ourselves these questions in an attempt to give order and meaning to our life. Paul explains in this passage that the Bible was given to us to help us. By reading the Scriptures we can find the answers to life's most difficult questions. Through the inspired Word of God, we can make sense out of our sometimes chaotic existence.

? What is a recent lesson or important truth that you have learned from the Bible?

? How would you explain to an unbeliever that the message of the Bible is just as relevant today as it was when it was written?

? What portion of Scripture do you find especially challenging at this point in your walk with God? Why is this a challenge for you?

? Do you feel it is important for a Christian to memorize Scripture? Why or why not?

? Tell about a time when you were depressed or upset and a passage of Scripture helped you.

COMBINED READINGS
Lamentations 1:1—Ezekiel 11:25
Philemon 1:1—Hebrews 6:20
Psalm 101:1–105:36
Proverbs 26:20–27:2

BIBLE MEMORY CHALLENGE
Lamentations 3:22-23
Hebrews 1:1-4
Psalm 103:13-14
Proverbs 26:23-26

POP QUIZ

OT: What gave the Israelites hope in such a desperate time? (Lam. 3:19-27)

OT: What did the scroll that Ezekiel ate taste like, and what did it mean? (Ezek. 3:1-3, 10-11)

OT: Where did the Spirit take Ezekiel, and what did Ezekiel see? (Ezek. 8:1-18)

OT: Why did the Lord tell the man in linen to put a mark on the foreheads of some of the people? (Ezek. 9:3-10)

NT: Why did Paul write a letter to Philemon? (Philem. 1:8-12)

NT: How has God spoken to us in these final days? (Heb. 1:1-3)

NT: Why did Jesus become a human being—made of flesh and blood? (Heb. 2:14-15)

NT: Why must we continue to mature in the Christian faith? (Heb. 5:11-14)

Psalms: Why did Joseph spend time in prison? (105:17-19)

Proverbs: Why should you not trust smooth-talking people? (26:23)

This Is a Warning

topic: Responsibility

reading: Ezekiel 3:1-27

verse: If good people turn bad and don't listen to my warning, they will die. If you did not warn them of the consequences, then they will die in their sins. Their previous good deeds won't help them, and I will hold you responsible, demanding your blood for theirs. (Ezekiel 3:20)

*I*f the people back in Judah continued in their sins, they and their land and cities would be destroyed by Nebuchadnezzar's armies. If, on the other hand, they turned to God, they would be spared. God would hold Ezekiel responsible for his fellow Jews if he failed to warn them of the consequences of their sins. All people are individually responsible to God, but believers have a special responsibility to tell others the consequences of refusing or failing to trust in Christ. If we refuse to witness to others or try to hide our faith from those around us, God will hold us responsible. This should motivate us to begin sharing our faith with others—by both word and deed—and to avoid being callous and unconcerned about them.

? In what situations is it most tempting for you to remain silent about your faith?

? Why do many of us view witnessing as an option, not a responsibility?

? What can we do to become more sensitive to the spiritual needs of those around us?

? In what situations is it most difficult for you to confront people about sin in their lives?

? What have you found to be an effective way for opening up conversations about religious beliefs?

? What changes are you ready to make in the way you share your faith with others?

COMBINED READINGS
Ezekiel 12:1–23:49
Hebrews 7:1–10:39
Psalm 105:37–109:31
Proverbs 27:3-13

BIBLE MEMORY CHALLENGE
Ezekiel 18:20, 23
Hebrews 9:27-28
Psalm 106:6
Proverbs 27:5-6

POP QUIZ

OT: Why did God tell Ezekiel to pack for a journey? (Ezek. 12:1-11)

OT: What was God's response to the proverb "The parents have eaten sour grapes, but their children's mouths pucker at the taste"? (Ezek. 18:1-4)

OT: How could the people of Israel escape judgment? (Ezek. 18:30-32)

OT: How did the people respond to God's command that they get rid of their idols? (Ezek. 20:7-8)

NT: Why did Abraham give Melchizedek, King of Salem, a tenth of his battle spoils? (Heb. 7:4-5)

NT: What priest lives forever to intercede for us? (Heb. 7:24-25)

NT: What happened to the old covenant when Jesus introduced the new covenant? (Heb. 8:13)

NT: What will Christ's purpose be when he comes again? (Heb. 9:28)

Psalms: Why did God save the Israelites by taking them out of Egypt? (106:7-8)

Proverbs: How does a prudent person handle the future? (27:12)

The Gift of Life

topic: Forgiveness

reading: Hebrews 9:11-28

verse: In fact, we can say that according to the law of Moses, nearly everything was purified by sprinkling with blood. Without the shedding of blood, there is no forgiveness of sins. (Hebrews 9:22)

*W*hy does forgiveness require the shedding of blood? This is no arbitrary decree on the part of a bloodthirsty God, as some have supposed. Rather, there is no greater symbol of life than blood; blood keeps us alive. Jesus shed his blood—gave his life—for our sins so that we wouldn't have to experience spiritual death, which is eternal separation from God. Jesus is the source of life, not death, and he offered his own life so that we might live. After shedding his blood for us, he rose victorious from the grave and proclaimed victory over sin and death. He has also given us the Holy Spirit to help us deal with present sin, and he promises to return and raise us all to eternal life in a world from which sin is banished.

? Why do you think this basic element of our faith, Christ's death, makes some people uncomfortable?

? What images come to mind when you hear the phrases "blood sacrifice" and "cleansed with blood"?

? How would you explain to an unbelieving friend why Christ had to die and shed his blood for him or her?

? If Christ has sacrificed so much for us, why are we so prone to stray from him?

? How can the blood of Christ motivate you to be more consistent in your walk with God?

COMBINED READINGS

Ezekiel 24:1–38:23
Hebrews 11:1—James 2:17
Psalm 110:1–117:2
Proverbs 27:14–28:1

BIBLE MEMORY CHALLENGE

Ezekiel 36:25-27
Hebrews 11:1
Psalm 110:1-7
Proverbs 27:17

POP QUIZ

OT: When Ezekiel's wife died, what did God tell Ezekiel to do? (Ezek. 24:15-17)

OT: In what ways would God judge Egypt for not helping Israel? (Ezek. 29:6-15)

OT: What was Ezekiel's responsibility as the watchman for Israel? (Ezek. 33:1-9)

OT: What did the bones represent in Ezekiel's vision of the valley of dry bones? (Ezek. 37:1-14)

NT: What is faith? (Heb. 11:1)

NT: Why does the Lord discipline us? (Heb. 12:5-11)

NT: How should we respond when trouble comes? (James 1:2-4)

NT: If you want wisdom, what should you do? (James 1:5-8)

Psalms: For what kind of people does life go well? (112:5-9)

Proverbs: Why are friends important? (27:17)

The Definition of Faith

topic: Faith

reading: Hebrews 11:1-6

verse: What is faith? It is the confident assurance that what we hope for is going to happen. It is the evidence of things we cannot yet see. (Hebrews 11:1)

*E*ach of us exercises a measure of faith every day. Even the atheist cannot say that he or she is without faith. When we sit in a chair, we have faith it will not break. When we walk into a store, we have faith that the construction crew made the building sturdy so that the roof won't fall on us. Faith is one of the most common elements in our existence. Without it, we would cease to function effectively. For Christians, faith is necessary for salvation, for our daily spiritual existence, and for the hope that some day we will spend eternity with the Lord Jesus in heaven. We all have faith in something. Make sure yours is based on Christ, and ask God to help your faith grow.

? How is the faith necessary for our salvation different from the faith necessary for our daily spiritual existence? How are they similar?

? When is it foolish to have too much faith in something?

? Tell about a situation when you had faith in something or someone and it failed you. How did that experience impact you?

? Can we have faith in something we do not trust? Explain your answer.

? In what things do you have the greatest faith? Why?

? What could you do today to help strengthen your faith?

COMBINED READINGS
Ezekiel 39:1—Daniel 2:23
James 2:18—1 Peter 4:6
Psalm 118:1–119:80
Proverbs 28:2-14

BIBLE MEMORY CHALLENGE
Daniel 2:20-22
James 4:7-10
Psalm 118:22-26
Proverbs 28:13-14

POP QUIZ

OT: Why did God say he would destroy Gog and Magog? (Ezek. 39:1-8)

OT: Why did the east gate in the outer wall of the Temple always have to remain closed? (Ezek. 44:1-3)

OT: What diet did Daniel and his friends eat during their training in Babylon? (Dan. 1:11-16)

OT: What special aptitudes and abilities did God give Daniel and his friends? (Dan. 1:17)

NT: Why is it important to do good deeds as well as have faith? (James 2:26)

NT: Why should we humble ourselves before God? (James 4:6-10)

NT: Why must we be holy? (1 Pet. 1:15-16)

NT: How can we follow Christ's example in times of suffering? (1 Pet. 2:21-24)

Psalms: What kind of people are happy, and why? (119:1-3)

Proverbs: Why should we confess our sins instead of covering them? (28:13)

Admit Your Faults

topic: Confession

reading: James 5:13-18

verse: Confess your sins to each other and pray for each other so that you may be healed. The earnest prayer of a righteous person has great power and wonderful results. (James 5:16)

*C*hrist has made it possible for us to go directly to God for forgiveness, but confessing our sins to one another still has an important place in the life of the church. If we have sinned against an individual, James instructs us to ask him or her to forgive us. If our sin has affected the church, we should confess it publicly. If we need support as we struggle with a sin, we can confess it to those whom we know would provide prayerful support. If, after confessing a private sin to God, we still don't feel his forgiveness, we may wish to confess that sin to a fellow believer and hear him or her assure us of God's pardon.

? If you confess your sins to God, why should anyone else have to know about them?

? Why are we afraid to admit our faults to each other?

? How might your friends react if you started freely admitting your sins to them? How open should we be about our sins?

? In what circumstances is it most beneficial to share your doubts and failures with others?

? How can confession to another person be healing for us?

? With whom would you feel most comfortable speaking openly about your sins?

COMBINED READINGS

Daniel 2:24–11:1
1 Peter 4:7—1 John 3:6
Psalm 119:81–121:8
Proverbs 28:15-28

BIBLE MEMORY CHALLENGE

Daniel 4:35
1 John 1:8-9
Psalm 119:133
Proverbs 28:20

POP QUIZ

OT: To whom did Daniel give the credit for interpreting the king's dream? (Dan. 2:28)

OT: Why did King Nebuchadnezzar threaten Daniel's three friends with death, how did they respond, and what happened to them? (Dan. 3:14-18)

OT: What message did a hand write on the wall of Belshazzar's palace? (Dan. 5:1-28)

OT: Why was Daniel thrown in the lions' den, and what happened to him there? (Dan. 6:1-23)

NT: Why should we be glad about trials? (1 Pet. 4:13-14)

NT: How do we know that the Bible was not "made up" by men? (2 Pet. 1:16-20; 1 John 1:1-4)

NT: What happens naturally if we are living in the light of God's presence? (1 John 1:7)

NT: Why should we not focus on earthly possessions? (1 John 2:15-17)

Psalms: What will happen to those who love God's law? (119:165)

Proverbs: What's wrong with trying to get rich quick? (28:22)

Biblical Guidance

topic: Guidance

reading: Psalm 119:132-136

verse: Guide my steps by your word, so I will not be overcome by any evil. (Psalm 119:133)

*I*n this passage the psalmist is affirming the importance of understanding God's law. Many times believers pray for the Lord's direction in their lives while at the same time neglecting the very biblical absolutes necessary for guidance. These biblical absolutes begin with the Ten Commandments. They are truths from God's Word that never change. The first step in understanding God's will and making right decisions is knowing God's law and practicing what the Bible teaches.

? Which of the Ten Commandments do you feel our society most flagrantly violates? Why?

? In what ways do you think the church is being soft on a particular aspect of God's law at this time?

? What are some examples of biblical absolutes? biblical principles? personal convictions based on the Bible?

? What is a lesson you learned when you disobeyed one of God's laws?

? Explain a time in your life when following God's commands protected you from evil.

COMBINED READINGS

Daniel 11:2—Joel 3:21
1 John 3:7—Revelation 1:20
Psalm 122:1–128:6
Proverbs 29:1-18

BIBLE MEMORY CHALLENGE

Joel 2:28-32a
1 John 5:14-15
Psalm 123:1-4
Proverbs 29:5

POP QUIZ

OT: Whom did the Lord tell Hosea to marry? (Hos. 1:2)

OT: What results from planting the good seeds of righteousness? (Hos. 10:12)

OT: What "army" invaded the land of Israel? (Joel 1:6-7)

OT: What people and city will remain forever? (Joel 3:20-21)

NT: How can you tell the difference between those who are Christians and those who are not? (1 John 3:10)

NT: How was Jesus revealed as God's Son? (1 John 5:6-8)

NT: What should we do when another Christian sins? (1 John 5:16)

NT: Why should we watch out for those who would deceive us? (2 John 1:7-10)

Psalms: How secure are those who trust in God, and why? (125:1-2)

Proverbs: What happens when you flatter someone? (29:5)

Choose to Love

topic: Relationship

reading: 1 John 4:7-21

verse: Dear friends, let us continue to love one another, for love comes from God. Anyone who loves is born of God and knows God. (1 John 4:7)

*E*veryone believes love is important, but we usually think of it as a feeling. In reality, love is a choice and an action. God is the source of our love for others: He loved us enough to sacrifice his Son for us. Jesus is our example of what it means to love others; everything he did in life and death was supremely loving. The Holy Spirit gives us the power to love others, even those who are difficult to love. God's love always involves a choice and an action, and our love should be like his.

? Which do you think is the more powerful motivational force: love, hate, fear, or greed? Why?

? What is the relationship between knowing God and loving others?

? Why is it sometimes easier to love God than other Christians? Why is it sometimes easier to love other Christians than God?

? How does God's love motivate you to treat other people?

? In what tangible way can you demonstrate your love for God?

COMBINED READINGS

Amos 1:1—Micah 7:20
Revelation 2:1–7:17
Psalm 129:1–135:21
Proverbs 29:19–30:6

BIBLE MEMORY CHALLENGE

Micah 5:2
Revelation 3:20
Psalm 133:1-3
Proverbs 30:5-6

POP QUIZ

OT: What did God want to see from the people instead of "show and pretense"? (Amos 5:21-24)

OT: What nation lived in a mountain fortress, and why would God punish it? (Obad. 1:2-4, 10-14)

OT: To what city did the Lord tell Jonah to go, and how did Jonah respond? (Jon. 1:1-3)

OT: From what small village in Judah would a ruler of Israel come? (Mic. 5:2)

NT: What complaint did God have against the church at Ephesus? (Rev. 2:4)

NT: How does Jesus respond to lukewarm people? (Rev. 3:15-16)

NT: What does Jesus promise to do for those who open the door to him? (Rev. 3:20-21)

NT: Who is worthy to break the seals on the scroll? (Rev. 5:2-5)

Psalms: What benefit does harmony among brothers bring? (133:2-3)

Proverbs: Why should you control your temper? (29:22)

Praise in Heaven

topic: Salvation

reading: Revelation 7:9-17

verse: They were shouting with a mighty shout, "Salvation comes from our God on the throne and from the Lamb!" (Revelation 7:10)

*P*eople may try many methods to remove the guilt of sin—good works, intellectual pursuits, and even casting blame. However, the crowd in heaven was praising God, saying, "Salvation comes from our God." Salvation from sin's penalty can come only through Jesus Christ. Only his blood can remove the guilt of our sin. Though there is nothing we can do to pay God back, we owe him a continual debt of gratitude.

? How did you feel when you came to the realization that God's gift of salvation was free?

? What have you seen people do to try to get rid of their load of guilt?

? What hinders people from clearly seeing their need for salvation?

? Why do some people insist on trying to earn their way into heaven?

? How can you more fully thank God for his gift of salvation?

COMBINED READINGS
Nahum 1:1—Zechariah 5:11
Revelation 8:1–14:20
Psalm 136:1–142:7
Proverbs 30:7-23

BIBLE MEMORY CHALLENGE
Nahum 1:7
Revelation 14:13
Psalm 139:23-24
Proverbs 30:7-9

POP QUIZ

OT: What is better than relying on wealth? (Hab. 2:4-5)

OT: What would the day of the Lord be like? (Zeph. 1:14-18)

OT: What message did the Lord send through the prophet Haggai? (Hag. 1:3-8)

OT: Why was Jeshua, the high priest, given new clothes? (Zech. 3:1-7)

NT: How did the people who had not been killed by plagues respond? (Rev. 9:20-21)

NT: How was the woman who had given birth to the child protected from the dragon? (Rev. 12:13-17)

NT: Who worshiped the beast? (Rev. 13:8)

NT: Who were standing with the Lamb on Mount Zion? (Rev. 14:1-5)

Psalms: How did David respond to the thought that God is everywhere and knows everything about him? (139:1-7, 23-24)

Proverbs: Why should you never slander a coworker? (30:10)

The Avenger

topic: Revenge

reading: Nahum 1:2-8

verse: The Lord is a jealous God, filled with vengeance and wrath. He takes revenge on all who oppose him and furiously destroys his enemies! (Nahum 1:2)

*I*n this day of lawsuits and incessant demands for legal rights, waiting patiently for God to avenge us when we are wronged seems almost impossible. When someone hurts us deeply, our natural reaction is to seek revenge or repayment of some kind immediately. But this is not our right. Only God has the right to carry out vengeance because he is perfect, he justly punishes those who wrong others, and he does not seek revenge for selfish motives. So what should we do when someone wrongs us? We should forgive that person and leave vengeance to the Lord. As Paul writes, the Lord "will repay those who deserve it" (Romans 12:19). Give up your desire for revenge, and trust God to punish those who hurt you.

? What is the difference between poetic justice and God's vengeance?

? Why is it hard to have patience and trust God to deal justly with those who hurt you?

? Why would you avenge yourself rather than leave that to God?

? When did you consciously decide to forgive someone who injured you in some way instead of seeking revenge? What influenced your decision?

? In what way do you need to let go of a desire for revenge against an individual or group?

COMBINED READINGS

Zechariah 6:1—Malachi 4:6
Revelation 15:1–22:21
Psalm 143:1–150:6
Proverbs 30:24-31

BIBLE MEMORY CHALLENGE

Malachi 2:16
Revelation 20:11-15
Psalm 145:8-13
Proverbs 31:8-9

POP QUIZ

OT: Why would Jerusalem one day mourn? (Zech. 12:10-14)

OT: How had the priests of Malachi's day despised the Lord's name? (Mal. 1:6-8)

OT: What did God urge married couples to do, and why? (Mal. 2:14-16)

OT: What prophet would come before the great and dreadful day of the Lord, and what would be the result of his preaching? (Mal. 4:5-6)

NT: Who were standing on the crystal sea mixed with fire, and what were they doing? (Rev. 15:2-4)

NT: How should we prepare ourselves for Jesus' return? (Rev. 16:15)

NT: At the final judgment, how will people be judged? (Rev. 20:11-15)

NT: What does God promise for those who live in the New Jerusalem? (Rev. 21:1-4)

Psalms: For what should we praise God? (150:2)

Proverbs: Who should we speak up for? (31:8-9)

The Second Death

topic: Hell

reading: Revelation 21:1-8

verse: "But cowards who turn away from me, and unbelievers, and the corrupt, and murderers, and the immoral, and those who practice witchcraft, and idol worshipers, and all liars—their doom is in the lake that burns with fire and sulfur. This is the second death." (Revelation 21:8)

The lake of fire is the final destination of the wicked. When God's judgment is finished, he will cast Satan, demons, death, and hell into the lake of fire, along with all of those whose names are not recorded in the Book of Life because they have not placed their faith in Jesus Christ. The second death referred to in this verse is spiritual death, meaning either eternal torment or destruction. In either case, it is permanent separation from God. This is the future that all people who reject Christ can expect.

? Do you think Christians who fall into the sins of corruption, immorality, or lying are in danger of going to hell? Why or why not?

? How does the reality of hell make you feel about witnessing to your unbelieving friends?

? Why are we afraid of telling unbelievers about hell?

? How can we be truthful in our witnessing and at the same time avoid using "scare tactics" to get our unbelieving friends to trust in Christ?

? What changes could you make to improve your witnessing?

SAVE $10.00

...when you purchase a New Living Translation Bible
(genuine leather)
The same fresh and readable NLT text that makes
reading *The One Year Bible* so enjoyable, is also available in a
"regular Bible" format. For personal study or to bring along to chur

This coupon may be redeemed only at locally owned

For your nearest location call:
1-888-4-PARABLE
or visit www.parable.com